*The Voices of Matthew Arnold*

# The Voices of Matthew Arnold

AN ESSAY IN CRITICISM

By W. STACY JOHNSON

Published for Smith College
by the YALE UNIVERSITY PRESS
New Haven and London

# Preface

THIS ESSAY is a critical study of Matthew Arnold's poetry, attempting to indicate when and how Arnold was able to succeed as a poet. It is not primarily, like Louis Bonnerot's *Matthew Arnold Poète* (Paris, 1947), a psychological study of Arnold the man nor, like Lionel Trilling's *Matthew Arnold* (New York, 1939), an examination of his ideas; neither does it comprise the results of original research into the sources and circumstances behind Arnold's poetry, as Chauncey B. Tinker's and Howard F. Lowry's *The Poetry of Matthew Arnold* (New York, 1940) does. These works, and others, have been drawn upon only when they seemed relevant to the interpretation and judgment of Arnold's poems considered as works of art.

For aid in the preparation and publishing of this book, I am grateful to the donors of the Elizabeth Edwards Chace Fund of Smith College, to the college Committee on Studies in Literature, and to the Ford Foundation. I am indebted also for various helpful gestures to Professor Manuel Durán of Yale University, to Professor Frederick Gwynn of Trinity College, Hartford, and, for permission to consult unpublished manuscript material, to the Yale University Library.

Finally, I owe debts of gratitude to my colleagues at Smith College who read and criticized the essay in typescript, Professors Newton Arvin, Elizabeth Drew, and Alfred Young Fisher, and Dean Helen Randall; to Professor A. Dwight Culler of Yale University for his very useful suggestions and his encouragement; to Professor J. R. Derby, under whose direction my interest in Arnold was developed; and to Professor Hyatt Waggoner of Brown University, my teacher and critic from the freshman year until now. The errors and absurdities that persist in these pages are here in spite of the good offices of these good friends.

W. S. J.

Northampton, Massachusetts
August, 1960

# Contents

NOTE ON TERMS USED AND PASSAGES QUOTED

*VOICE.* Although there are a good many voices from out of the blue, or the depths, described and recorded in the poetry of Matthew Arnold, this essay is mostly concerned with other modes in which the poems seem to speak. I use the word *voice* somewhat as T. S. Eliot does when he considers *The Three Voices of Poetry* (London, 1953). The first of Eliot's voices, that of the poet speaking to himself, is more or less equivalent to soliloquy; the second, the voice of the poet speaking to an audience, is represented by Arnold in what I call his oracles; the third, the dramatic voice, is heard in dialogue and sometimes, at least, in monologue. I do not agree with Eliot that the second voice necessarily dominates in dramatic monologue, even though that may be true of Browning, to whom he refers, and whose mannerisms never let us forget that, whatever his *persona,* the poet is the speaker. Of the narrative voice, which is neither the intrusive *I* of a commentator nor the dramatic *I* of a character, Eliot gives no account. He does, however, suggest that there may be fewer or more voices than three, and that these may be intermixed in any one poem—as they are, certainly, in Arnold. In fact, the use of such categories is to some extent a matter of impression, and justified only as it applies to particular poems and poets.

For instance, my distinction between the terms *soliloquy* and *monologue* is somewhat arbitrary, if not without precedent in conventional usage: in writing of Arnold's soliloquy, I mean such a speech as the reader must imagine being uttered aloud by a person who is alone, a speech that is overheard by the reader-as-auditor; monologue, on the other hand, is the speech of a fictional person not to the reader but to a fictional auditor or auditors whose presence the speaker implies. It is always dangerous to suppose that poets mean literally what they say, but I am inclined to associate Arnold's own conscious point of view more closely with that of his unidentified *I* than with those of characters like Balder and the forsaken merman.

*TONE.* I take this word to mean the expression in writing of an attitude toward the subject treated, the equivalent in this limited sense of a tone of voice. Ironic or pathetic, emotional or detached, controlled or shrill, the tone of a poem derives from the poet's style, especially his diction. By *tone* I do not mean, as some writers do, the expression of a writer's feelings about his audience. The voice in a dramatic monologue may indicate a distinct attitude toward the person being addressed, but in such a work, to the extent that this is true, that person becomes part of the speaker's subject. When, however, a writer seems to treat his reader with respect or disgust, with high seriousness or playfulness, the result is ordinarily what I should call preaching or advertising rather than poetry. It strikes me that this calculated appeal to or attack upon an imagined reader is what weakens, for example, much of Ezra Pound's verse and some of Matthew Arnold's prose—weakens them as works of art rather than as works of propaganda.

The text to which all quotations from Arnold's poetry refer is that of Chauncey B. Tinker and Howard F. Lowry, *The Poetical Works of Matthew Arnold* (New York, 1950).

# 1. Arnold as a Victorian Poet

IN SPITE OF THE variety in styles and opinions that makes Victorian literature so easy to misrepresent by any generalization, there are certain tendencies which the English poets who flourished between 1830 and 1880 have in common to distinguish them from their successors and their predecessors—more especially from their predecessors. These post-Romantic tendencies, so to speak, result not from common assumptions about the nature of man and of his world but rather from a common consciousness of questions to be asked and perhaps to be answered, of uncertainties which have to be met or carefully avoided. Tennyson and Browning, Swinburne and Hopkins, Morris and Patmore, Dante Rossetti and Christina Rossetti make up in some ways an oddly assorted list, but for all of them the questions of a man's proper relation with other men, and with God or the Universe, are peculiarly serious: whether as mystics, reformers, debaters, or dreamers, they are aware that what they say or imply on these hardly avoidable subjects will be accepted by some and challenged by many of their intelligent fellows. There is no common Victorian doctrine, no single predominant "new movement," not even a single great division with lines clearly drawn, no crucial battle of orthodox against Puritan, ancient against modern, classic against Romantic. In fact, with these Victorian writers, we enter what seems very much like the complex modern world, except that the thoughtful men in this world, including prophets and poets, are intensely earnest and often honestly baffled by its dizzying incoherence, its multitude of parts and possibilities.

The change from a Romantic to a Victorian sensibility can be illustrated in several ways, if we examine a few instances from each of the two periods, choosing some specimen short poems: Wordsworth's "The Solitary Reaper," Coleridge's "The Rime of the Ancient Mariner," Shelley's "Epipsychidion," and Keats's "La Belle Dame sans Merci" from the one group, and from the other, Tennyson's "The Lady of Shalott," Browning's "Love Among the Ruins," Arnold's "Dover Beach," and Swinburne's "Hertha." We can, of course, make comparisons that cut across these groups: "La Belle Dame" and "The Lady of Shalott" are both vaguely medieval in setting, both suggest ballad narrative in their development and use of a refrain or echo, and both are apparently symbolic. "Epipsychidion" and "Hertha," in a quite different vein, are sustained by expansive, even cosmic imageries. But what qualities, if any, seem to differentiate the two groups?

Perhaps the most obvious of distinctions, that between an "aesthetic" or personal subject and one which is moral or social, is also the most dubious, or at least the most easily exaggerated. Nevertheless, we observe that the faery beauty of La Belle Dame seduces Keats's knight and the singing of the solitary reaper entrances Wordsworth; that Shelley refers to music at the beginning of his "Epipsychidion," the only substantial unity of which is provided by recurrent references to the natural and artificial harmonies perceived by the poet; and that Coleridge's mariner is saved not by any simply physical or moral action but through an aesthetic reaction: he beholds the thousand slimy water snakes by the light of the moon

and, realizing their beauty, blesses them. Whatever the main subjects of the four Victorian poems, they are not, in the same sense,
the experiences of beauty. "The Lady of Shalott" contrasts a life of
aesthetic contemplation, an inner life, with the gesture of commitment to the world outside, the world of Lancelot. Whereas Keats's
knight is destroyed by the wiles of his beautiful lady, Tennyson's
beautiful lady is destroyed by a glimpse of her knight: life and love
are the victims of beauty in the one poem, life and beauty are the
victims of love in the other. Browning's "Love Among the Runis,"
however, and Arnold's "Dover Beach" hold that "love is best"—
better than the pomps of the world and better than the worship of
Nature—as if to justify the lady's action. And finally "Hertha" has
to do not with beauty (or love) but with truth; in it, Swinburne is
a preacher and a moralist. But already we are in danger of distorting
the facts. We have to remember that if "beauty is truth" for Keats,
then truth is beauty, too; in general, the English Romantics insist
upon the cognitive and moral elements involved in aesthetic per-
ception. Furthermore, some of the later Victorians, including Rossetti, consciously turn away from social and moral subjects. It is not
with the Romantics but with the later Victorians that the idea of
"Art for Art's sake" flourishes.

So far, so commonplace, no doubt. But less obvious and perhaps
more revealing than a partial shift in subject matter is the changed
quality of metaphor and setting in Victorian poetry. With a wider
range of reference, we might compare the predominant imagery of
the Romantics, imagery of growth, interfusion, and constancy which
assumes the organic wholeness of Nature, with the imagery of the
Victorians, which tends toward polarity and tension rather than
unity. The symbols remain, but they are pictured with more intense ambivalence, so that Victorian flowers and fruits can be lovely
and false, Victorian sunlight brilliant and painful, the Victorian sea

magnificent and bitter; in an echo of Byron's apostrophe to the ocean as an "image of eternity," Browning's Don Juan (in "Fifine at the Fair") finds that mirror of nature alien, too, an "old briny bitterness." And precisely this ambivalence occurs again and again in Arnold's evocations of the "sea of life," including "Dover Beach."

Ambivalence of imagery is one evidence of the Victorian reaction to Romantic assumptions about man and nature. In the Romantic poems cited there is either an implicit or a stated relationship between a dominant human figure and his natural environment—the vale, the creatures of the deep, the pathetically silent birds and still lake, the stars, moon, waters, and heavens that reflect a poet's emotions. But in the Victorian examples, natural objects are in several ways foreign to men: the images of the outside world are associated with the destroying of the inner life in Tennyson, are contrasted with the ruins of human pride in Browning, become quite cold and alien in Arnold; even in Swinburne's allegory, Hertha dwarfs every human figure and far transcends all human time, in spite of the bombastic and egalitarian yoking of Earth and abstract Man. What Swinburne has to insist upon, the Romantics assume, but they also assume the primacy of human spirit in the ultimate oneness of man and Nature.

Another matter of some significance has to do with point of view. "La Belle Dame" and "The Ancient Mariner" are narratives into which the poet does not enter except as story-teller; the language of the poem is too simple and strange in the one instance, and, in the other, too clearly dramatic—it is the language of a character—for us to suppose that Keats or Coleridge is here speaking his mind or literally describing his experience. Both Keats and Coleridge do that elsewhere, of course, as Wordsworth and Shelley do in "The Solitary Reaper" and "Epipsychidion." We have no doubt when we read works such as these that the poet himself is speaking. In either dramatic or personal verse, as a matter of fact, the Romantic point of view is likely to remain unambiguous. We do have doubts, however, about the Victorian point of view, not in the narrative "Lady of Shalott," which is at most a very indirect expression of Tennyson's mind, but in "Love Among the Ruins," "Dover Beach," and "Hertha." As Professor Smidt has observed, there is a category of Victorian poems which falls somewhere between the dramatic and the direct, the method of which is "diagonal" or oblique, employing such projected voices as those of Browning's shepherd, Arnold's seaside lover, and Swinburne's earth goddess.[1] Even in dramatic poetry, when characters have opinions (and characters in Victorian poetry often have firm opinions) we are inclined to associate them with the poet's point of view: Browning is blamed for Pippa's optimism and Tennyson for the defense of war uttered in *Maud*. And although readers seize upon such expressions too often and too easily, the poets may be said to invite some confusion by failing to contain or qualify the gay and ranting voices.

This ambiguity of voice in some Victorian poetry, one has to suppose, results from the poets' uncertainty about their own opinions and thus about how fully they can enter into the voices of the preacher, the casuist, the skeptic, and how firmly they can control the competing attitudes expressed; it results in a poetry capable, when it remains within dramatic bounds, of embodying psychological ambiguities, of doing justice to internal tensions, but a poetry often marred, too, by falseness of tone, by the weakly vague or the merely strident pronouncement. Perhaps in itself it matters very little what Tennyson believed the woman's role in marriage should be when he wrote *The Princess;* what does matter is that the tone of the poem falters and fails disastrously so that no vantage point

1. Kristian Smidt, "Points of View in Victorian Poetry," *English Studies*, *38* (Feb., 1957), 1–12.

defines the whole work, and we remain uncertain, in many passages, whether a comment is ironic or highly serious.

Uncertainty of tone, at best an ambiguity and at worst a false blustering, generally characterizes Victorian and not Romantic poetry. (It is likely in a modern poet to be intensified, becoming conscious irony.) The slightest hint of an ambiguous tone can be caught in "Love Among the Ruins" and "Dover Beach": how are we to judge a self-satisfied lover's rejection of distant earthly glories and the wooing of a disillusioned intellectual who falls back on love when all else has failed? There is not so much an ambiguity as a careful avoidance of any striking tone in "The Lady of Shalott," with its morbid beauty and its deadly sunlit out-of-doors. But in some passages of "Hertha" we can hear the shrill tone of the vague and insistent seer—the vaguer, the more insistent.

The extent to which Victorian poets feel called upon to leave their palaces of art and play a vatic role in society has been shown by E. D. H. Johnson, who suggests the difficulty any Victorian artist must find in speaking with his own voice.[2] Professor Johnson's contrast between subterranean and public art may be, however, a little too sharp; the greatest difficulty for the Victorian writer is to know what his own voice is. It is not only the poet whose work is affected by this difficulty: the great era of prophetic poets and poetic prophets is almost unanimous in its desire for a largely impersonal voice, whether its source be revelation, ecclesiastical authority, the world-soul, physical science, or some other eternal "not ourselves" which makes for knowledge and perhaps for righteousness. But along with this desire goes an ineluctable urge to examine and project the writer's personality. Carlyle preaches against self-conscious-

2. E. D. H. Johnson, *The Alien Vision of Victorian Poetry* (Princeton, 1952); see especially the concluding chapter, in which the thesis of the book is emphatically stated, and p. 218, for the phrase used here.

ness in a barely disguised and intensely self-conscious autobiography, Newman's apologia for his submission to an authoritative order is a very personal self-defense, and both the candid Mill and the falsifying Ruskin are profoundly concerned with the accounts of their histories. The examination of one's own life and opinions to be certain of what one is and what one believes, this seeking for the image of oneself, is distinctly Victorian when it is combined with an apparently impersonal manner. In *Sartor Resartus* as in "The Two Voices" and "Empedocles" there is a dialogue of the mind with itself, a barely disguised search for the poetic *me* by the poetic *I*.

Distinctly Victorian, too, and closely related to the search for personal identity, to a faltering of the personal voice and an ambiguity in dramatic voices, is the sense of a need to be converted, to be wholly persuaded of the Truth and so made whole. It is difficult now to speak of such a sense without seeming to be ironic; whereas an earlier and less evangelical age, generally secure in its beliefs, would see no necessity for conversions, our insecure age cannot ordinarily accept the possibility of conversions. But thoughtful Victorians were likely to think conversion to some form of Truth necessary, and to hope at least that it was possible. The period is rich in documents of conversion, some certainly genuine like Newman's, some largely fantasy like Carlyle's and Tennyson's, some subtle and partial like Mill's. *Sartor Resartus,* Mill's *Autobiography* and Tennyson's "Two Voices" approximate a single emotional pattern, moving from No to Yea, from a feeling of emptiness and isolation, a loss of faith in any value, through a crisis to the affirmation of life in the form of a new conception, a new faith. Three of the four poems in our sample, without following this pattern, suggest the Victorian need to make a declaration of faith or of faithlessness, to utter an everlasting No or an everlasting Yea: Browning and Swinburne affirm their general beliefs and Arnold states his very general rejection of a belief.

Rather than underlying and supporting the poems, as Wordsworth's and Coleridge's do, the faiths are given as propositions, in each instance, at the climax of the poem.[3]

The combination of self-questioning and the need for conviction, the need for an objective manner, affects, then, both the technique and the tone of Victorian poetry: if, with the use of monologue and other forms of dramatic indirection, a point of view is sometimes still ambiguous, it is because the poet has to enter in largely and cannot enter in fully to characters' declarations and decisions. Mill's remark about the early Browning's intense and morbid self-consciousness may have had some effect in producing a poetry more like the kind Mill would prefer, a poetry that seems to be overheard, but the result transforms without destroying the poet's intense self-consciousness.

All of these tendencies of Victorian poetry can be found in Matthew Arnold, and he is aware of most of them. His subject matter is moral and (although his method is not) philosophical. He produces both declarative and dramatic verse, and in both kinds the

3. On the Victorian "Pattern of Conversion," see the chapter with that title (Chapter 5) in Jerome Buckley, *The Victorian Temper* (Cambridge, Mass., 1951), pp. 87–108.

Victorian conversions are not all religious in nature, but almost all of them, like the various pronouncements of faith made in this period, have something to do with attitudes toward time, that "miracle," as Carlyle puts it, "a thing to strike us dumb—for we have no word to speak about it" (although he goes on to speak about it in some thousands of words). Of the four Victorian poems cited here, three (Browning's, Swinburne's, and Arnold's) deal specifically with ideas of time and change; and only "Hertha" suggests the Romantic sense of a constant life immutable in mutability. The conflict between a mystical conception of time as illusion and a rationalist conception of time as the only reality is perhaps the most basic conflict in the literary mind of the period. Mill and other progressives incline to the rationalist view, Carlyle tends uneasily to the mystical, Arnold vacillates; Newman and Hopkins, of course, as Catholic Christians, insist upon the reality and value of both temporal and eternal things.

control of his tone is a serious problem; ambiguity is a strength only
in the more dramatic kind. He understands his need to find his own
voice as well as the need to see steadily. And he understands the
difficulty in doing so, in following his own true line or realizing
what he calls the buried life. At the same time, Arnold can be moved
by the oracular voices of others, especially when he tires of his unending and irresolute dialogue of the mind. He is never able to accept
the Christian gospel as his father did, for whom it was "an ever-
living oracle furnishing to every age . . . precise rules, principles, and
laws of conduct," and, like Arthur Hugh Clough, he is repelled by
the voice of mechanistic science; indeed, none of the various oracles
he hears can ever quite fully persuade him, as "The Voice" in his
poem cannot, the voice that

> Blew such a thrilling summons to my will,
>> Yet could not shake it;
> Made my tost heart its very life-blood spill,
>> Yet could not break it—

but he waits on, as his scholar-gipsy does, for the true oracle, and
hopes for the conviction that would mean conversion.[4] More skeptical than Clough, he never entirely abandons this hope that a new
Moses may descend from the cloudy mountain-top of Truth.

Arnold's susceptibility to prophetic voices and finally his sense of

4. The remark about Thomas Arnold's accepting the gospel as an oracle
was made in a letter by Bonamy Price, one of Arnold's assistant-masters at
Rugby. The letter is included in Arthur Stanley's *Life* (London, 1904), p. 193,
and is quoted by Walter Houghton in his *Victorian Frame of Mind* (New
Haven, 1957), p. 146.

Clough uses the imagery of mountain and voice in "The New Sinai." Although inner voices of doubt or reassurance and mysterious but persuasive
voices of good counsel are not uncommon in the Victorian poets—there are
the "Two Voices" of Tennyson, for instance—Matthew Arnold would seem
to have more than his share of them.

duty to a prophetic office pull him away from his poetic line, no doubt, but if he felt no such tension he would not be a serious Victorian poet, and he could not have written "The Forsaken Merman" and "Dover Beach." W. H. Auden hears the "jailor's voice" in his criticism and blames the death of his poetic strain on misplaced reverence for a father's word; but, however profound the Sohrab-and-Rustum conflict may be in Arnold's life, his inability to praise his own disordered world and his turning in search of order to prose criticism result less from filial piety than from a Victorian set of mind which works to produce his virtues as it does to narrow and sometimes to flaw them.

The flaws are many. In refusing to be limited by the sentiment of love or by the religious sentiment, Arnold limits the range of his sensibilities. In committing himself, or partly committing himself, to a too pragmatic and public view of the poet's duties he cuts himself off from interesting and important kinds of poetry—the kind, for instance, that the metaphysicals and some moderns write, in which a confrontation of the self by the self can be resolved in irony. For better or worse, he is in the Victorian situation, and Victorian questions about the definition of man in relation to God, to nature, to human society, and to himself press upon him to make his unbeliefs unnerving and his view of serious literature both too severe and too simple.

But the virtues are there, too, and Arnold's seriousness, quite alien to pomposity, is the first of these. The primary aim of this essay is to examine the virtues of his poetry, with all its moral earnestness, its ambiguity in point of view and tone, its combining of self-consciousness and objective forms. Some of it is excellent poetry, not in spite of its being Victorian or because of its being Victorian, but in the particular modes of excellence that Arnold's environment allows.

## 2. The Voice Oracular

FRET NOT YOURSELF to make my poems square in all their parts, but like what you can my darling. The true reason why parts suit you while others do not is that my poems are fragments— i.e. that I am fragments, while you are a whole; the whole effect of my poems is quite vague and indeterminate—this is their weakness; a person therefore who endeavored to make them accord would only lose his labor; and a person who has any inward completeness can at best only like parts of them; in fact such a person stands firmly and knows what he is about while the poems stagger weakly & are at their wits end. I shall do better some day I hope—meanwhile change nothing, resign nothing that you have in deference to my oracles; & do not plague yourself to find a consistent meaning for these last, which in fact they do not possess through my weakness.[1]

In this paragraph of a letter to his favorite sister Arnold offers a valuable if slightly exaggerated piece of self-analysis. Arnold the critic often measures against such criteria as those of distinctness and

1. *Unpublished Letters of Matthew Arnold,* ed. Arnold Whitridge (New Haven, 1923), pp. 18–19.

integrity just the tendencies of his age which Arnold the poet
cannot successfully resist. He decries the English habit of "using
poetry as a channel for thinking aloud," he complains that "we have
poems which seem to exist merely for the sake of single lines and
passages," and he turns, in "these bad days," to the un-Victorian art
of Sophocles, "who saw life steadily and saw it whole."[2] But in his
own work the "thinking aloud" is often unrelieved, and his intellectually ambitious pieces are often worth preserving merely for
the sake of a line or a few phrases. The sonnet on Sophocles' whole
and steady vision, for instance, introduces itself in a peculiarly unsteady voice: the tributes to Homer and Epictetus are unutterable,
un-English attempts at classical concision—

> Who prop, thou ask'st, in these bad days, my mind?—
> He much, the old man, who, clearest-soul'd of men,
> Saw The Wide Prospect, and the Asian Fen,
> And Tmolus hill and Smyrna bay, though blind.
>
> Much he, whose friendship I not long since won—

and so on. And yet the poem concludes rhythmically in several of
Arnold's happiest lines, with eloquent praise for the "singer of sweet
Colonus, and its child."

Arnold's self-criticism might be taken to suggest that there are
really two weaknesses, although they derive from the same final
irresolution, which would set his poetry in contrast with that of the
Greek, his ideal; he has neither steadiness nor wholeness, he is both
faltering within the limits of one work and inconsistent in the body

2. See *Unpublished Letters,* p. 17; and the 1853 Preface, included by Chauncey
B. Tinker and Howard F. Lowry in their edition of *The Poetical Works of
Matthew Arnold* (London, 1950): Arnold's complaint about poems' existing
"for the sake of single lines," probably intended as a criticism of the "Spasmodic" poets, appears on page xxiii of that edition.

of his work. The impression of his inconsistency from poem to poem must strike anyone who reads much more of Arnold than "Dover Beach," for it is the inconsistency of a man debating with himself. But the more serious fault is the vitiating uncertainty of tone within the poems. It is a fault implied, perhaps, by the poet's often engaging in debate rather than dialectic. The tension that characterizes a certain kind of verse, that is, results not from a series of antitheses working according to a single logic but rather from the opposition of ultimate attitudes, which, when they appear distinctly as attitudes, are likely in one way or another to be negated by their opposites. Thus the poet adopts a shrill over-insistent tone in making half-hearted assertions or blurs his language or leaves his dialogue uncompleted.

This criticism applies especially to the category of poems that Arnold calls oracles[3] (the verse of thinking aloud), but the best of these are not quite ruined by uncertainties. In fact, even the apparent inconsistencies among these oracles are sometimes less a result of confusion about ideas than they seem to be, for they amount to differences between the hyperbolic expressions of opposed moods. Often, following Seneca and the Stoic school, the poet regards the physical world as a pattern for man and uses "nature" as an ethical term; at other times he looks upon this world as lacking a moral order, as alien to human aspirations. The sonnets "Quiet Work" and "In Harmony With Nature" ("To an Independent Preacher") both deal with this subject of man's relation to nature, a subject that Arnold is almost always writing about, but they represent two quite different emotions: the poet's desire to withdraw from the turmoil

3. The term *oracle* is used in this essay as Arnold uses it, to mean simply an authoritative pronouncement, an inspired saying, rather than an obscure and ambiguous message delivered by a visionary, the sense in which the word is applied to Tennyson by Robert Preyer in "Tennyson as an Oracular Poet," *Modern Philology*, 55 (May, 1958), 239–51.

of human society and his fear that he will lose his humanity in so withdrawing.[4] The first sonnet is an attempt to unify two duties in learning one lesson, and it is an affirmative poem:

> One lesson, Nature, let me learn of thee,
> One lesson which in every wind is blown,
> One lesson of two duties kept at one
> Though the loud world proclaim their enmity—
>
> Of toil unsever'd from tranquility!
> Of labour, that in lasting fruit outgrows
> Far noisier schemes, accomplish'd in repose,
> Too great for haste, too high for rivalry!
>
> Yes, while on earth a thousand discords ring,
> Man's fitful uproar mingling with his toil,
> Still do thy sleepless ministers move on,
>
> Their glorious tasks in silence perfecting;
> Still working, blaming still our vain turmoil,
> Labourers that shall not fail, when man is gone.

In striking contrast is the poet's tirade against the "independent preacher," possibly against himself.

> 'In harmony with Nature?' Restless fool,
> Who with such heat dost preach what were to thee,
> When true, the last impossibility—
> To be like Nature strong, like Nature cool!

4. This alternation of desire and fear is one form that a central conflict in Arnold's work takes: the conflict between an urge toward practical action and an urge toward disinterested criticism, examined by E. K. Brown in *Matthew Arnold: A Study in Conflict* (Chicago, 1948). In the first chapter of this study, Brown sums up the objections to Arnold's apparent inconsistencies, including the inconsistency between his critical precepts and his poetic practice.

Know, man hath all which Nature hath, but more,
And in that *more* lie all his hopes of good.
Nature is cruel, man is sick of blood;
Nature is stubborn, man would fain adore;

Nature is fickle, man hath need of rest;
Nature forgives no debt, and fears no grave;
Man would be mild, and with safe conscience blest.

Man must begin, know this, where Nature ends;
Nature and man can never be fast friends.
Fool, if thou canst not pass her, rest her slave!

We may have misgivings about the central term "Nature" in both of these poems.[5] ("What pitfalls there are in that word," Arnold exclaimed to Clough after he had tumbled into several.) If we take it to mean the out-of-doors physical world, and apparently it excludes man in the sense it is given here, then we might expect to get at it in one or two specific forms. But there is not a vivid image in either poem, unless one tries to picture the "lasting fruit" that "outgrows/ Far noisier schemes," and that conception hardly bears up under scrutiny. What natural fruit lasts? How does fruit outgrow schemes? Even less defensible is the major half of the crucial assertion in the first sonnet, that physical nature, wind and all, works quietly. Of course these are literal objections, of course noise and silence are metaphorical equivalents for emotional turmoil and calm; but the metaphors fail of that literal truth which the evocation of a particular silent force, animal, vegetable or mineral, would give and which terms like "labour" and "labourers" do not in themselves

5. Arnold's various uses of the word are compared by Joseph Warren Beach in his *Concept of Nature in Nineteenth-Century English Poetry* (New York, 1936), pp. 397–405.

suggest. What the sonnets lack is the literalness of the best kind of poetry, and they lack that quality because "Nature" is an idea the poet is unable to test against the experience of nature. He may hope for but he cannot perfectly imagine a peaceful ministry in the world, a natural labor which has an aim.

The rhetorical structure of "Quiet Work" is effected by its series of appositives, relative clauses, and participial phrases, moving, as they qualify, toward an oracular ending—an ending assertive in its form but involving negative elements: man's turmoil is blamed, his life is described as transient, and the final implication is that his labor may fail where Nature's "shall not." In fact, it is unclear just what is being affirmed, what the anonymous laborers succeed in. Nevertheless, the word that begins the sestet is "Yes," and the sense of this conclusion is, if hazy, still affirmative. In the other sonnet there is a series of contrasting assertions, parallel clauses that break, often at a medial caesura, into antitheses, and the effect is one of contrasts and contradictions: the sense of the sestet, finally, is an answer to the first four words of the poem, the answer "No." (But the strength and coolness referred to in the fourth line qualify this answer, too.) In both sonnets too much weight is put upon adjectives and very abstract nouns, but the more serious fault in the second is a shrillness of tone: the two uses of *fool* and the exclamation marks are so excessive for the subject that the poet's voice sounds too loud, sounds a little false.

As for the contrast between these two poems, it amounts to one of mood and emphasis: whatever the natural world lacks of true peace and help for human pain—to use the language of "Dover Beach," which the second sonnet anticipates—that world seems strong and silent in both poems; in both poems man is noisy and restless, nature cool and unfeeling. The poet has tired of human feelings in the first mood, but in the other he asserts a need for emotion, as if he were anxious about the possible loss of conscience, fear, and desire. Even so, the difference between his comparing two orders in one place and opposing them in another does not amount to a change in his definitions of man and nature. The poems express a conflict between distinct attitudes toward moral involvement and disinterestedness, because these ideas are so ambivalent to Arnold that he cannot succeed, when he writes about them, in clearly choosing one over the other. The fault with these sonnets, then, is not simply that they cancel each other out, but rather that each one very nearly defeats itself; they represent the slight blurring, in one instance, and, in the other, the stridency of tone that result from internal conflict neither resolved intellectually nor controlled by a sufficient use of poetic indirection.

And yet these two sonnets are poems, and not without value: each has its own structure and each speaks through its own voice. Dim and forced though the voices sound, they are at worst unsteady rather than incoherent. The failures that often occur when Arnold engages in thinking aloud instead of creating a story or celebrating an object or a person can be illustrated with any one of several other sonnets that do not deserve to be defended as more than fragments of critical verse. Some of these are fragments not only in conflict one with another, not only vague or half-hearted, but incoherent in that they seem to be forced into an irrelevant "poetic" form. In the sonnet to George Cruikshank and the two addressed "To a Republican Friend" (Clough), the poetic form is less awkward than that of the sonnet on Sophocles, but it is arbitrary, so that an allusive phrase like "Dian's horn," a bright line like "France, famed in all great arts, in none supreme," or a fleeting image like the "Mountains of necessity" acts only as ornamental distraction. In such pieces the idea itself, so blurred and botched, seems valueless. The Cruikshank piece asserts that men can and do torture and destroy each other but that this is the worst they can do, and the exclamation tempts one to reply, What worse would you have? And one is tempted again to call the message to Republican Clough, that the city of God is not built in a day, fine words and temporizing. These things might better have been put in prose; in verse, they are talked out with neither style nor urgency.

Arnold rarely succeeds in purely rhetorical verse (in the sense of an oration, using rhetoric to persuade) for he is not persuaded of the truths that he wishes intermittently to hold. In fact, he often appears to be unwilling or unable to define his truths. He can play with terms like "Nature" and "earth," "light" and "law," as he does in "Religious Isolation," but he will not often take them either literally as symbols or metaphorically as counters for distinct ideas; he will not, that is to say, provide a full enough literal or metaphorical context to define them. In some of his shorter pieces, then, the syntax expresses a conflict, but the ideas and sympathies involved in the conflict are not quite specified. When they are specified, when Arnold can pose clear and serious alternatives in his intellectual verse, and not vague or partial terms, he finds it all but impossible to choose between them.

He cannot choose, for example, at the end of "In Utrumque Paratus." The virtue of this poem is that it presents a fairly distinct either/or: either a Neo-Platonic idealism that isolates man from the physical world of seeming or a pan-materialism that unites him with all things and makes his unique humanity itself a seeming, an illusion. The first of these philosophies would imply man's loneliness in a world of trivial appearances:

> Thin, thin the pleasant human noises grow,
>     And faint the city gleams;
> Rare the lone pastoral huts—marvel not thou!

> The solemn peaks but to the stars are known,
> But to the stars, and the cold lunar beams;
> Alone the sun arises, and alone
>   Spring the great streams.

The alternative philosophy implies a negation of man:

> Oh when most self-exalted, most alone,
>   Chief dreamer, own thy dream!
> Thy brother-world stirs at thy feet unknown,
> Who hath a monarch's hath no brother's part;
> Yet doth thine inmost soul with yearning teem.
> —Oh, what a spasm shakes the dreamer's heart!
>   '*I, too, but seem.*'

The reasonable clarity of the terms in this poem, the use of Plotinus' fountain and stream of ideal reality, and the reversal in the meanings of sleeping and waking, so that human consciousness is represented as an awakening in the first half and as dreaming in the second, all provide a certain firmness to these lines. But the poem cannot fulfill the promise of its title, "In Either Case, Ready," which is the promise of a unifying conclusion. We can hardly tell how to be in either case ready, for the two philosophies demand contrary attitudes and courses of action.[6] Although the work does not quite break into equal parts, a deep crack in the middle leaves its unity at best a

6. For a more complete explication and criticism of the poem from this point of view, see *The Explicator*, *10* (May, 1952), Item 46.

Professor A. Dwight Culler suggests that the image of the mountain in this poem, symbolizing Arnold's intellectual position by suggesting a relationship both with heaven and with earth (the ideal heights, perhaps, and the literal plain), indicates how he is "in either case ready." And the title probably is intended to imply the need for combining a disinterested mind with a sympathetic heart, self-sufficiency with modesty. But it seems questionable that the poem itself, without its title, would lead a reader to these conclusions.

fragile one. So, while the elements of an interesting and even a moving poem are here, the final unifying control, the resolution implicit or explicit, is lacking. Each of the halves of "In Utrumque Paratus" is introduced by an *if,* and we end with two *ifs.* With the use of that word Arnold indicates his lack of any assured basis for the production of wholly satisfactory—or satisfactorily whole— philosophical poetry.

Even when Arnold's treatment of ideas in the form of verse has a certain value, that value is qualified as the assertive voice is muted by a lack of faith, whether a religious faith or faith in common experience. These are the facts of which Arnold, with his critical intelligence, is aware when he analyzes his own "staggering" verses and deprecates the use of poetry for speculation. And this awareness, this self-critical intelligence, is asserted in his poetry as well as in prose criticism; passages and whole poems can be read as oblique self-analysis, as reactions against his own tendency to abstract and intellectualize. One such poem is the sonnet "Written in Butler's Sermons," which introduces Arnold's use of land and ocean as symbolic of the human and non-human natures. A skeptical comment on the "vain labour" of the searching intellect, the poem celebrates man as an ultimately mysterious being, as "God's harmonious whole." Although it is not clear whether "man's one nature" means one personality conceived as a total *Gestalt* (rather than as an aggregate of Butler's instincts, affections, and so on) or whether it is some sort of human over-soul (or, in this imagery, under-soul), these lines quite clearly imply the superiority of the human spirit which

> rays her powers, like sister-islands seen
> Linking their coral arms under the sea,
> Or cluster'd peaks with plunging gulfs between.

Weakened by the "or," the ending is nevertheless distinctly metaphorical; it represents the turning away from a flatly abstract vocabulary of "Affections, Instincts, Principles, and Powers."

Another sonnet which can be read as a commentary on the poet's own dangerously explicit personal and intellectual involvement in his art is "Shakespeare," Arnold's finest poem in this form; the imagery here is that of magnitude and distance, and (as in "Quiet Work") of silence beyond sound.

> Others abide our question. Thou art free.
> We ask and ask—Thou smilest and art still,
> Out-topping knowledge.

An explanation of this poem has to begin with the question of what our question is. The most obvious question which most other great men in modern history submit to and which Shakespeare does not, is biographical, the question of what he really thought and did. But if the poet out-tops knowledge, he transcends it. We might say that he transcends the possibility of being known in the way a wholly revealed mind—the mind of the philosopher, for instance, which makes itself explicit—can be known, can be mastered. Perhaps the essence of the poet's genius, to put it another way, is not communicable: his peaks are beyond our view, he "spares but the cloudy border of his base/ To the foil'd searching of mortality." Freedom, silence, and the "heaven of heavens" which is the atmosphere of the mountain-top are opposed to the tolerating of questions asked, to the noisy questioning itself and to the mortal sphere. The genius, apparently, disdains to make direct pronouncements upon Life and his own life (the formula applies to Shakespeare if not to Dante or to Goethe); more than our lack of knowledge about dates and places, then, it is the silence of Shakespeare on such matters, his refusal of a specifically moral and prophetic role, which the poem judges to be better, because this silence allows him a different role. The ending of the sonnet makes the point beautifully:

> All pains the immortal spirit must endure,
> All weakness which impairs, all griefs which bow,
> Find their sole speech in that victorious brow.

The immortal spirit must endure pain, and it is endurance rather than asking and probing (the "searching of mortality") which characterizes the undying part of man; but within the silence of the bard there is a speech that reveals, and changes in revealing, the tragic and pathetic flaws, weakness and grief. The heightening and dignifying rhythm of these lines, along with the diction, suggest a transformation of pain, of bowing and impairment, into the victory of art. Arnold's oxymoron of silent speech is followed by another paradox, as the voice of the bard is embodied in his "victorious brow"—and this is a crucial phrase. For, easily as the poem seems to read, these final lines are both complex and ambiguous: "all pains" are narrowed to "sole speech," and the immortal spirit that endures them may be Shakespeare's, as the speech is, or the human spirit in general; but in any case, the "victorious brow," combining the original imagery of the poem (this is the brow of the "loftiest hill") with a suggestion of Shakespeare's forehead, can be taken to imply the mind of a poet whom we know not through any pronouncement or picture of him that would answer our trivial questions, but in his quiet work, in the form of dramatic poetry.[7] In spite of the slightly

7. Paull F. Baum provides a survey of various possible interpretations for the poem and his own paraphrase, including this reading of the last lines: "The conflict between [Shakespeare's] humanity and the immortal spirit within him is visible only in his features, i.e., not in his plays." This sense, as Professor Baum observes, would give the sonnet a "general unity," but it would also seem to make its meaning perverse: it would require our understanding Arnold to say that the author of *King Lear* does not give voice to

dubious magnificence of its hill-and-clouds imagery and the sentimental inaccuracy of its Emersonian line ("self-school'd, self-
scann'd," and so on), the poem comes to be largely redeemed by
its difficult and memorable conclusion.

A comparison of this poem with the sonnet "Written in Emerson's Essays," an interesting if less familiar work, suggests how much
more positively Arnold can give voice to the greatness of the distant
past than he can to the contentions of the immediate present. Although both poems have to do with men of genius, one pictures a
genius silent above the world, the other a genius speaking in and to
the world. The sonnets have in common an implicit criticism of
thinking aloud in poetry; for the one on Emerson reveals the plight
of a philosophizing artist who speaks out to a "dead, unprofitable
world" which, far from searching, will not hear the "voice oracular"
or will not believe the message heard. When one recalls Arnold's
reference to his own oracles, this criticism may seem double-edged.
Furthermore, while the poem begins in the tones of an enthusiast
chiding this world, there are quotation marks around the speech,
and in the second quatrain Arnold represents his situation as a dramatic one: the world smiles at his voice and passes by, "As though
one spake of life unto the dead." Those smiles are full of "bitter
knowledge" which would contradict his Emersonian optimism:

----

pains the immortal spirit must endure, to weakness and grief, in his plays,
that his looks show such pain but his poetry does not. Rather than accept this
reading, I would prefer to think that "victorious brow" is "a very forced
metonymy" for "successful poetry springing from the brain behind it." But
the poem is, after all, more obscure than it should be, for all the beauty of its
ending. Once again Arnold does not quite commit himself to either of two
positions, to Shakespeare idolatry or to a larger view of art, with the result
that, as Professor Baum comments, his skill appears to be "not above re-
proach." See Baum's *Ten Studies in The Poetry of Matthew Arnold* (Durham,
N.C., 1958), pp. 3–13.

> Yet the will is free;
> Strong is the soul, and wise, and beautiful;
> The seeds of godlike power are in us still;
> Gods are we, bards, saints, heroes, if we will!—
> Dumb judges, answer, truth or mockery?[8]

Ironically, these potential gods are silent. In spite of Emerson's assurances, most men cannot, or will not, be bards, saints, or heroes. The ironic ending is made possible by the use of quotation, confrontation, monologue which cannot become dialogue. Whereas the Shakespeare sonnet, after indulging in Emersonian reflections on the literary giant as a self-sufficient man, is partly saved from blandness (if not from obscurity) by its paradoxical language, this sonnet is saved from flatness by its dramatic method.

The first of these sonnets moves from questioning to victorious stillness, the second moves from proclamation to questioning, but for each poem the end is silence. So it is too for Arnold's Empedocles; the questioning voice of the Emerson sonnet is a voice more like that of Empedocles, the alienated questioning philosopher, than that of Callicles, the singer who (in the words of Auden's poem) finds a whole world to celebrate. This Empedoclean voice is heard frequently in Arnold's debate with himself, sometimes evoking the very elemental imagery of "Empedocles on Etna." In a number of shorter pieces, for instance, the image of the silent sea provides a setting, either literal and symbolic or metaphorical, that makes the

8. In an earlier draft of the sonnet, contained in the Yale manuscript, Arnold describes this response to the "voice oracular" with lines more sharply critical of Emerson's optimism: after the world only smiles at his prophet's message, the poet's joy (first word was "dream") is fled, "so scornful seemed that smile, so strange, so full/ Of bitter knowledge." See, for a full transcription of this version, the commentary on *The Poetry of Matthew Arnold* by Chauncey B. Tinker and Howard F. Lowry (New York, 1940), p. 27.

verse more particular, less abstractly intellectual. This oceanic image for the natural life of things, eternally in flux and always one, allows the poet to show man's relation with the elements, the most attractive and at the same time the most ambiguous of which—a link "between the inanimate and man"—is water.[9] But the ambiguity of his water imagery, while it can be a source of strength for Arnold as it is in "The Forsaken Merman," does not always make for metaphorical consistency: his mixed feelings about stream and ocean can also be a source of vagueness and vacillation. The poet can debate inconclusively about an image, as he can about an abstraction, and this is what happens when he discourses on metaphors or makes metaphorical assertions instead of describing things and allowing his imagery to imply its significance. Because neither Arnold nor the reader is obliged to choose for himself between Margaret's and the merman's worlds, it is possible to appreciate the demands of both, as it is to accept the terms of the conflict and its dramatic resolution in irresolution. When the poet tries to make a philosophical or moral choice between the sea of nature and the land of society, the conflict left unresolved is likely to be a contradiction in metaphorical terms rather than a tension held between contrary valuable images and actions, since it is a *diction,* a saying-so, with which he begins. Or the saying-so, again, may simply be vague and unconvincing. So, while there is at least as much of interest in "A Summer Night," "Self-Dependence," "The Youth of Man," and "The Fu-

9. Arnold's word is not "link" but "Mediator." He uses the phrase in a letter to Clough, written from Switzerland, which is printed by Howard F. Lowry in *Letters of Matthew Arnold to Arthur Hugh Clough* (London, 1932), p. 92. This water imagery, especially the imagery of sea and island and of sea and ship, occurs in Clough's poetry almost as often as in Arnold's, and there are sometimes striking similarities between the two poets' uses of it. A perhaps exaggerated argument for the importance of these similarities is made by my piece on "Parallel Imagery in Arnold and Clough," *English Studies,* 37 (Feb., 1956), 1–11.

ture" as there is in most of Arnold's short poems of ideas, we have to scrutinize them for what qualifies their value as much as for what constitutes it. We have to distinguish the voice of the oracle or debater from that of the narrator or lyricist.

Like Empedocles, the speaker in "A Summer Night" suffers from a thirst which seems at first to be unquenchable: a thirst not now for bliss so much as for peace, the peace of "unpassionate" skies. He is aware of his own vacillating nature, *"Never by passion quite possess'd/ And never quite benumb'd by the world's sway,"* unsure of his ability to feel deeply or to give up his feelings. Not in the worldly city, he knows, nor in the prison of habitual affairs and petty passions, the prison of day-to-day time, can he find peace. But in doing as he likes, in breaking out of that prison to sail free on "the wide ocean of life," he faces the dangers of madness: that way, in the impetuous struggle toward "some false impossible shore," toward a utopia or a personal salvation, there is only shipwreck. "Is there no life, but these alone?/ Madman or slave, must man be one?" No, the poet answers himself, a man can take courage from the untroubled heavens and work in tranquility. But the question is more striking than the vatic answer; and Arnold's picture of a "pale master on his spar-strewn deck," the madman sailing abroad on the ocean of life, is more memorable than his inspirational last lines. The terrible sense of this picture is that a man's will and spirit are destroyed by time and the nature of things as surely as his life is. Finally, the moral seems to be that man is to take nature, not will, for his guide, that he cannot sail "where'er his heart/ Listeth." But whether nature, here, means only physical nature or something more is not quite clear.

In "Self-Dependence," however, a poem the title of which would seem to contradict this moral, the oceanic nature is clearly said to lack any human characteristics. Like "A Summer Night," this poem begins as a soliloquy and becomes an oracle, with the utterance of an "air-born voice." In the extreme statement of an essentialist, as against any existentialist, view of life, the voice denies that man can create his personality by making decisions. What certainly commends this view to the speaker of the poem, what recommends the prophetic voice, is one person's weariness with the effort to define himself morally, the effort to find an image of what this human creature is who stands unique in a strange and threatening landscape —or seascape.

> Weary of myself, and sick of asking
> What I am, and what I ought to be,
> At this vessel's prow I stand, which bears me
> Forwards, forwards, o'er the starlit sea.

The human voice in this and in the second stanza is authentic and moving. But in the third stanza the tense shifts from present to past, from "I stand" and "I send (a look of passionate desire)" to "I cried"—and the cry is answered. It is as if the speaker has to give distance to his uncertainty, putting it in the past in order to provide an answer, to imagine that the Voice has indeed spoken. The answer, the oracle, is a Stoic moral: to depend upon oneself is to depend upon the nature that is one with stars and sea. If a man is to know peace, he must live as they do.

> Unaffrighted by the silence round them,
> Undistracted by the sights they see,
> These demand not that the things without them
> Yield them love, amusement, sympathy.

A person finds his true self, his best self, by denying his ordinary self, and apparently by denying desire and relationship. Because this conclusion is rather too much of an airy sermon, too easily received and too little proved by the "myself" of the first stanza, the rest of the poem carries none of the impact of that opening. The speaker's weariness takes a form more memorable than the philosophy of a disembodied voice.

A third poem that uses the image of a ship in the ocean is "Human Life," and in it the same philosophy is even more explicit. The poem does, it is true, begin with a reference to the mortal's "heavenly Friend," and the tone is sternly moral, but finally it is an unknown nature which sweeps man away from the "unsuiting consort" and the attractive coast "on life's incognizable sea."

> No! as the foaming swath
> Of torn-up water, on the main,
> Falls heavily away with long-drawn roar
> On either side the black deep-furrow'd path
> Cut by an onward-labouring vessel's prore,
> And never touches the ship-side again;
>
> Even so we leave behind,
> As, charter'd by some unknown Powers,
> We stem across the sea of life by night,
> The joys which were not for our use design'd;—
> The friends to whom we had no natural right,
> The homes that were not destined to be ours.

Destiny and "natural right" appear to be identical in these lines, so that a man cannot, even if he wishes to, dominate the natural force that guides him; and neither, if the sea is "incognizable," can he understand that force. He can only realize that the sea of his environment isolates him from others. All of this is said in a consistently oracular tone, with no suggestion of personal feeling, so that the poem is a whole, a stoical sermon with no other voice intruding on the preacher's. If "Human Life" lacks internal tension, if the voice communicates no passion, no sense of real pain or sacrifice in its references to friends, to "joys," to "homes," and the "unsuiting consort," at least it competently versifies the proposition that the image of nature determines the image of man, and that man's relationship with the universe determines his relationship with other men.

It is not, according to "The Youth of Nature," a reversible proposition. Contradicting Romantic idealism, this poem asserts a beauty imbedded in things which is more than art or philosophy can reveal. It begins, nevertheless, as a lament for Wordsworth, who "lent a new life" to the mountains and valleys where he lived.

> These survive!—yet not without pain,
> Pain and dejection to-night,
> Can I feel that their poet is gone.

But the *persona* of the elegist, the *I* who mourns for Wordsworth, becomes more and more that of the critic and the questioner, until this voice is stilled by the mysterious voice of an oracle, a voice from the air which answers the speaker's questions:

> I heard, as men heard
> In Mysian Ida the voice
> Of the Mighty Mother, . . .
> The murmur of Nature reply—

The interpolation of this "higher strain" is not alien, of course, to the convention of elegy, but whereas Milton's Apollo and St. Paul, in "Lycidas," are given only passages of morality, Arnold's oracle takes up nearly half the poem, and concludes it, in lines which have none of the tender quality and persuasive elegiac tone of the first half. Once more the speech from out of the blue, or out of the depths, the speech of an all-encompassing *I* to *you* who "know not yourselves," repeats a Stoic conclusion: that Wordsworth's "lending of life" to physical nature was really the assuming of power to see; that pain and dejection are not felt by mountain, shadow and lake, which remain in their grandeur, alive and passionless, after the death of the seer. So Nature's voice assures us that the external world outlasts man and dominates him. The only implied and unanswered question is, again, whether man is part of this world or an orphan in the universe.

One answer, the Empedoclean answer, would be that the human consciousness is at best a temporary self-destructive freak in nature and at worst an eternal principle of pain, the single evil in an otherwise perfected and therefore amoral life of the elements. The answer in "The Youth of Man," personifying Nature as "mild and inscrutably calm," is perhaps more comfortable than that, but at last, in its pious tone, it is rather less comprehensible. This companion piece to "The Youth of Nature" reads like a prayer to the "Soul of the world," which comes in the last stanza to be identified with the soul that dwells in man as well as in all physical life. The poem might almost be called "Dover Beach Thirty Years After" (and, although it was published about fifteen years earlier, it may possibly have been written after "Dover Beach"). In lines that recall the last verse paragraph of the greater poem, a young couple speak of the realm of nature that lies before them like a land of dreams:

> she
> Hath neither beauty, nor warmth,
> Nor life, nor emotion, nor power.

With the Coleridge of "Dejection" they declare,

> Nature is nothing; her charm
> Lives in our eyes which can paint,
> Lives in our hearts which can feel.

But this view is rejected again by the poet and by the couple as they age, apparently on the assumption that the longevity of natural forms indicates their essential beauty and warmth. The poem ends with an echo of Solomon's injunction, "Remember now thy Creator in the days of thy youth."

> While the locks are yet brown on thy head,
> While the soul still looks through thine eyes,
> While the heart still pours
> The mantling blood to thy cheek,
> Sink, O youth, in thy soul!
> Yearn to the greatness of Nature;
> Rally the good in the depths of thyself!

This hortatory conclusion points a moral to the story of the old couple, but it is not very clear what there is to moralize about, what the particular results of being like Nature are and what "the good" amounts to. The question that vexes Clough and to which "Religious Isolation" is addressed, seems here to be begged, unless "good" is supposed in this poem to have not an ethical but some other significance. In "Morality" Arnold is uncomfortably conscious of the problem, and he imagines that Nature, if she is now without a moral law, once saw and felt "that severe, that earnest air" before she knew the "gauge of time." Still, if to be like Nature is to be amoral, to be without good and evil, as "Morality" would suggest, then "the good" in the ending of "The Youth of Man" is a curiously arbitrary term. The moralist would seem to be preaching with all but unnatural fervor the gospel of amoral Nature. But this interpreting of one poem by another, when both are the products of a writer who so often changes his mood if not his mind, is perhaps unfair; at most it indicates again the ambiguity for Arnold of such terms as "Nature" and "the good."

And, for all the dubious ambiguity of his language, it is clearly the difference between human mortality and the natural recurrence of forms, rather than the difference between moral man and the amoral inanimate, that the poet of the two "Youths" is mainly concerned with. His theme is man in time. This is the theme, too, of "The Future," in which the contrast between mortal man and the elements that outlast him is imaginatively realized.

The metaphorical, or, in this instance allegorical, elements of a river and, once more, a ship, make up the somewhat conventional substance of "The Future":

> A wanderer is man from his birth.
> He was born in a ship
> On the breast of the river of Time.

The poem is both a comment on the spiritual landscape of the present, this plain in which the river banks are hemmed by cities, and a fantasy of temporal fulfillment. In the first part the anapestic lines are hesitant rather than gliding as the river "sluggishly winds through the plain"; but at the end this rhythm is nicely modulated, especially in the exceptional fifth, fourth, and third lines from the last, which set up their own pattern of satisfaction.

> And the width of the waters, the hush
> Of the grey expanse where he floats,
> Freshening its current and spotted with foam
> As it draws to the Ocean, may strike
> Peace to the soul of the man on its breast—
> As the pale waste widens around him,
> As the banks fade dimmer away,
> As the stars come out, and the night-wind
> Brings up the stream
> Murmurs and scents of the infinite sea.

Like the river Oxus passage at the conclusion of "Sohrab and Rustum," these lines discover an end to conflict in oceanic peace— a consummation and a fulfillment of finite, unique, and partial forms, of human fragments, in the infinite whole. The symbol is eastern and mystical; it yields neither the practical and moral meaning that Thomas Arnold would demand of a parable nor quite the clear meaning of a strictly controlled allegorical figure. What, we may ask, happens to the ship of the second line when it reaches the sea? Is it an ocean-going vessel? Or does it now sink to the depths? And if man "wakes" on the stream of life, as the eighth line (like a passage of "In Utrumque Paratus") has it, what does he wake from, and what, in the ocean, go to? This water imagery is suggestive and it has some effect, no doubt, of mediating between the inanimate and man, as Arnold says; but unless the river and the ocean are more than elemental symbols, man is drowned in being received by the infinite powers. The conflict between conscious mortality and eternal substance can be resolved in this poem only by the poet's ignoring for the moment all these questions—questions which a symbolic narrative would not force upon us in any such precise sense but which are raised here by the declarative form and vatic tone. The result is a partial vision and a readable poem but a minor poem lacking the energy of forces realized and firmly held in tension.

"The Buried Life" is at once a less consistently interesting poem in itself than "The Future" (the imagery in it is illustrative and little developed) and a more complete statement of Arnold's thought. In it Arnold tries to imagine, as he cannot in his poems about Marguerite, a rare and difficult communion between persons normally isolated from each other. He tries to imagine a final answer to a recurrent question:

Alas! is even love too weak
To unlock the heart, and let it speak?
Are even lovers powerless to reveal
To one another what indeed they feel?
I knew the mass of men conceal'd
Their thoughts, for fear that if reveal'd
They would by other men be met
With blank indifference, or with blame reproved;
I knew they lived and moved
Trick'd in disguises, alien to the rest
Of men, and alien to themselves—and yet
The same heart beats in every human breast!

The speaker's desire, in the lines just before these, is to read in his beloved's eyes her "inmost soul." But as he proceeds he seems to be less concerned with her soul, dwelling upon "every human breast," and, finally, upon "our breast." So what begins as a love poem ends as a comment upon self-analysis. Perhaps a man can see his hidden self in his beloved's eyes and thus gain knowledge of the buried life, the underground stream of his own existence. For

Only—but this is rare—
When a belovéd hand is laid in ours,
When, jaded with the rush and glare
Of the interminable hours,
Our eyes can in another's eyes read clear,
When our world-deafen'd ear
Is by the tones of a loved voice caress'd—
A bolt is shot back somewhere in our breast,
And a lost pulse of feeling stirs again.
The eye sinks inward, and the heart lies plain,
And what we mean, we say, and what we would, we know.

A man becomes aware of his life's flow,
And hears its winding murmur; and he sees
The meadows where it glides, the sun, the breeze.

And there arrives a lull in the hot race
Wherein he doth for ever chase
That flying and elusive shadow, rest.
An air of coolness plays upon his face,
And an unwonted calm pervades his breast.
And then he thinks he knows
The hills where his life rose,
And the sea where it goes.

This conclusion, like the last lines of "The Future," is at least vaguely hopeful—vaguely, because a man only "thinks he knows." The natural and strengthening effect of what is taken for love in these lines may be only to turn one's eyes inward, but then the married couple in "The Youth of Nature," overwhelmed as they are by the world, derive no natural strength at all from their love: they make no plea, "Ah love, let us be true to one another," in the face of inanimate powers.

In at least one other place, however, a stanza in the poem "Progress," Arnold specifies the danger to man's affections and his moral sense posed by a sea-philosophy that makes no more of love than a means of self-knowledge. Obliged to discard the Christian faith, its law, and its symbols, the poem still echoes Empedocles' last prayer, "Quench not the fire within!"

> 'Bright else and fast the stream of life may roll,
> And no man may the other's hurt behold;
> Yet each will have one anguish—his own soul
>     Which perishes of cold.'

This is the third voice in the poem, the voice of the "old world"; the first voice is Christ's, the second that of the "new world," and the fourth and final strain is one from heaven itself, urging the validity of all religions. But the third voice is not so catholic, with its distinctly western concern for the "fire within" of feeling and of human sympathy; and in these tones the poet speaks his anxieties about the inhuman coldness of an ideal peaceful Nature. Whether the insight of this moment is compatible with that uncertain vision which concludes "The Buried Life," whether human relationships are compatible with wholeness and peace, is a question that remains unanswered. We can say only that the poet's vision of the river and the sea shifts and is modified from voice to voice.

In almost every one of these instances, the very personal tone of doubt, of need, of despair, is too painful for the poet to sustain; and so even the image of the sea, that recurrent and central image in Arnold's poetry, is not always enough to give objective form to the emotions communicated. So, time and again, it is not the identifiable *I*, the human speaker who dominates and concludes Arnold's account of human life in an ocean of natural change, of danger and mystery, but rather a desired oracle, a reassuring voice out of the sky or the sea itself, a voice that speaks of philosophy but not of experience.

Most of the later examples of Arnold's oracular verse were published together in the "New Poems" of 1867: sonnets and other short pieces, they are, with two or three exceptions, fairly uninteresting as poetry. "Palladium," however, is a graceful bit of allegorizing, and "Youth and Calm" (from a poem of 1852), ending once more with the words of "a voice" from within—

> *Calm's not life's crown, though calm is well.*
> 'Tis all perhaps which man acquires,
> But 'tis not what our youth desires—

carries more conviction than Arnold's stoical poems can.[10] We hear the same tone, neither hopeful nor stoically resigned, in "Growing Old":

> What is it to grow old?
>
> . . .
>
> It is to add, immured
> In the hot prison of the present, month
> To month with weary pain.

The triumph of time, man's loss of intensity with age, are always disturbing themes in Arnold; but here, caught in the very prison from which he once imagined an escape into the depths (in "A Summer Night"), the poet speaks most clearly, most sadly. Indeed, the tone is hardly oracular, for it carries in the precision and justness of its diction an unstrained certainty.

In "East London," "West London," "Anti-Desperation" (a melancholy title), "Immortality," "Worldly Place," and "The Divinity" there is little of such conviction, and the tone is mostly perfunctory rather than shrill or ambiguous. In these forms, Arnold's social and religious ideas seem rather ordinary and rather dull. Or, at worst, the critic's seriousness can quite overwhelm the poet's finer sensibility. A poet's serious thought, according to the sonnet entitled "The Austerity of Poetry," is "a hidden ground," like sackcloth under the Muse's gay apparel. But in this sonnet and in others of its kind, the ground is not hidden at all: so far from seeming gay and radiant, the Muse is all in sackcloth.

Finally, the last of Arnold's most ambitious oracles, "Obermann

---

10. "Youth and Calm" consists of the second paragraph of "Lines Written by a Death-Bed," lines which Professor Culler, following a suggestion of Louis Bonnerot, believes to have been originally a part of "Tristram and Iseult."

Once More," demands some notice: it lacks, perhaps, the concentration of his first poem on Obermann; perhaps it strains too hard
against the poet's despair to sound altogether convincing at the end;
but this attempt to rally the spirits at least indicates what it is that
Arnold wishes for, with sometimes feeble hope. Once again it is a
voice from afar—this time the voice of Sénancour's Obermann—
that speaks to the poet, filling sixty-four of the eighty-seven stanzas
in this poem with its evocation of the familiar water imagery and
with its desire for a new "common wave of thought and joy," a
wave which is to succeed Christianity ("the wave/ Of love"), and
to unite those men of good will who now live on island "blocks of
the past like icebergs." The voice of this vision, real or illusory, dies
away, the vision fades, and the poet awakes. But while it speaks the
voice is at least fervent and clear.

As we have observed, Arnold's voices are not always so clear.
The very slight poetical worth of some of his sonnets and other
short thoughtful poems is not finally altered by the fact that these
poems deal with serious matters and even suggest serious ideas, for
they do so incoherently. All that gives interest to pieces that are
blurred and fragmentary is the relationship between these exercises
in reflection and other poems which are more than that. For the
problems dealt with in the minor poems appear again in the major:
in narrative and dramatic works where they are confronted by the
lonely and reflective souls who people Arnold's imagined world,
and in purely dramatic and symbolic poems.

Most of Arnold's poems are in some sense problem pieces. The
basic and recurring problem is that of finding a valid image for man
in his world, whether the image of God's creature, of a very god,
or of an uncreated uncreating thing—the orthodox or the Romantic
or the naturalist image. Failing to settle on such an image, the poet
can only refuse and negate the idea of the distinct self, of which he

is painfully conscious. This problem takes the form of questions about man's relationship with his physical environment, nature, and his human environment, society, from both of which, without the image, he will seem to be isolated. And it takes the form of anxiety as to whether a person so isolated can know his world, his fellows, or himself, whether he can achieve any sort of knowledge. Even if Arnold states anxieties and hopes as fixed ideas, his commentators have always recognized that the mood of his poetry is the mood of doubt. He conscientiously doubts not only the Christian religion, which he never seems to take quite seriously except as poetry (he takes it more seriously that way than he might himself have supposed), but all the orthodoxies, idealist and materialist, Romantic and scientific. He alternately holds and attacks almost every possible Victorian position.

But critical thinking aloud in this sense is not the first, certainly not the only, business of the poet; uncritical Tennyson is a much less intelligent man and a greater poet than Arnold. Furthermore, Arnold's critical intelligence is clearest when he is writing his least consciously intellectual poetry. "The Forsaken Merman" makes a fuller and more acute analysis of the conflict between the idea of civilization and that of natural impulse than any of the short explicit verses; on any other point than this general theme, it would be absurd to compare that poem with the sermon on the "Independent Preacher": there is so much more than, but also (for that reason) so much more *of* 'general theme' in "The Merman."

The necessity of thinking aloud in the sonnets, rather than making an imaginative whole, is what often leads Arnold off his own poetic line, as he himself puts it when he is afraid of being distracted from a career of poetry. For his is the line that very few mid-Victorian poets can consistently follow, the line of the artist who, in the words of his 1853 preface, "creates, forms, and constitutes," rather than that of the seer who debates, submits, and concludes. In his admiration for the silence of Shakespeare and his doubts about the voice of Emerson, Arnold hints at this conclusion. There are such things as philosophical poetry and the union of oracle and artist, but because of the divisions and conflicts in the intellectual life of his age and the lack of clarity or system in any available synthetic view, almost any Victorian poet must find it difficult to be at once precisely philosophical and satisfactorily poetic. And yet, in the circumstances, he is peculiarly tempted, not to a polemics that replaces art but to a vagueness that undoes it. This is especially true, as Arnold knows, of a poet sensitive to general ideas.

Perhaps, even so, there is some psychological as well as public necessity for Arnold's thinking aloud and for his listening now and then to dim and distant voices which are not entirely convincing nor precisely located. Without "Butler's Sermons" and "Self-Dependence" we might have no "Dover Beach"; perhaps the thinking aloud and the questioning must be done, from time to time, for Arnold in better moments to succeed in his quiet work of writing whole poems rather than fragments.

# 3. Soliloquy

THE INTERNAL contradictions and inconclusiveness that weaken many of Arnold's short oracular verses have their source in a conflict between two needs, the need for faith in a moral order and the need for faith in some ultimate unity of things. When he sees the world from a moral point of view, as a social creature, Arnold is a dualist: he perceives that loving, suffering man and inanimate nature are distinct. But when he writes from his need for wholeness Arnold is, in dream or aspiration, a monist: he can imagine only one nature in the universe, ordering an apparent multitude of apparently self-centered, aimlessly colliding fragments. This combination of a traditional moral sense, allowing for evil or moral emptiness deeply imbedded in a fallen nature, with an eastern or transcendental faith, rather shakily held, does not make a firm ground for criticism. Whereas the Christian poet might see an ultimate triumph of the one Good (with its various manifestations) over the neutral as well as the negative, the deprived as well as the depraved, Arnold is sometimes obliged by his loyalty to the One to assume that truth transcends morality.

The problem has to do with time as much as with strictly ethical problems because, like Emerson and Carlyle, Arnold is mostly concerned with the immanence of truth and inclined to deny divine transcendence or the duality of finite and infinite. For him as for

Carlyle, the sense of time can be perplexing: time is an illusory mask over eternal wholeness, one of Arnold's voices must declare, the appearance of a river which is ultimately and really an ocean, and not the medium through which men define their characters and save their souls. And yet he can be struck, as he returns to the moral view, by a feeling of man's real temporal imprisonment which would lead him to deny that transcendental faith.

This poignant sense of man's imprisonment in time and his eternally frustrated impulse to transcend temporal (and moral) limitations fills Arnold's most personal poetry. In his soliloquies the precepts of Spinoza and the Stoics are likely to sound forced; the clearest voice, here, is the saddest voice. Indeed, the great strength of at least several among these poems which do not address an audience directly is that they require no inspiriting conclusions: a sermon or an oracle must seem to arrive at a fairly explicit end, but the soliloquy may end only with the uncertainty of its speaker. The integrity of such a poem is the integrity of a complex person, not that of a complex argument. Ideas are involved in Arnold's poetry of this kind, but in the best of it the reader is confronted with an *I* who gives voice to feelings, too, and almost always to the feelings of frustration and loss or uncertainty. The tone may be faintly ironic, like that of the final line in the sonnet on Emerson, posing a question. For the mode is more nearly dramatic, self-dramatizing even, than hortatory.

In the quasi-dramatic mode Arnold can often achieve an unequivocal point of view and tone of voice: he can come closer to achieving integrity. His quiet work is done by the submergence of a critical intelligence in the objective form that best expresses it; he manages in this way to pursue his poetic line and to give substance to those problems, those conflicts, which largely absorb him. In one rather slight but curiously interesting reflection of a mood, for instance, called "A Modern Sappho," the brevity of poor human love is given voice by a speaker located in time and place:

> Nothing stirs on the lawn but the quick lilac-shade.
> Far up shines the house, and beneath flows the river—
> Here lean, my head, on this cold balustrade!

And the conclusion, in the words of this lovelorn maiden, is only an Arnoldian comment on the passions given a personal form.

> I shall suffer—but they will outlive their affection;
> I shall weep—but their love will be cooling; and he,
> As he drifts to fatigue, discontent, and dejection,
> Will be brought, thou poor heart, how much nearer to thee!
>
>                   . . .
>
> Hast thou yet dealt him, O life, thy full measure?
> World, have thy children yet bow'd at his knee?
> Hast thou with myrtle-leaf crown'd him, O pleasure?
> —Crown, crown him quickly, and leave him for me!

Even Arnold's criticism of Romantic attitudes can be self-dramatizing rather than directly critical. Just as his Tennysonian Sappho turns away from a landscape of lilac and lawn, of river, music, and youth, so, with her weariness of fire and light, of Romantic passion and vitality, the poet himself turns away, in a more ambitious poem, from "The New Sirens." These are the embodiments of pure feeling who vacillate between hysteria and ennui; as Arnold suggests in his explanation to Clough, they appeal more to the spirit than to the flesh, for the poem is an animadversion on Wertherian–Byronic Romanticism in its extreme form.[1] To "enchanted lawn" and "darken'd palace rooms" their admirers come as exiles from the springs of knowledge, the silent mountains, and from the bright

1. *Letters . . . to Clough,* pp. 105–7.

and morning star—from intellectual, contemplative, and religious lives. They come from these fixed landscapes to which they have belonged, to a place of dimness and wavering forms, a place men create in their image and shape according to their fleeting desires.

The sirens of Romanticism, willing to think aloud, speak in disillusioned voices:

> Judgment shifts, convictions go;
> Life dries up, the heart dissembles—
> Only, what we feel, we know.

The details of their appearance and the setting in which they move reveal more about these sirens, however, than their voices do. The literal and metaphorical patterns of light and darkness, vitality and death, run through the poem so as to establish a unifying sense which the musing of these allegorical figures would not. They are seen first in shadow, then at sunrise, their eyes "heavenly," their brows "starred with dew"; and the speaker reflects that if the dawning failed to grow into daylight, if their joys were unexposed by the sun of noon to which a stronger hope attaches than to the wings of morning—if all this were so, the aposiopesis implies, the sirens could retain their charm for him. But their fitful life of emotion does not bear the common light of day. Once, we are told, they watched "for a purer fire," for some light more certain than the inner flame and less harsh than the ordinary sun, perhaps one that could unify the two in a humanized nature. But that hope is dead, and they have turned again and again to "some transient earthly sun," either some inner light of feeling or some object of desire, until they are self-centered and cut off from all that is natural. They are brilliant with a wholly artificial light and vivacity that "the sorrow-stricken day denies." The mood of the poem, for all this imagery of brilliance real and artificial, is a dark one that shrinks

from both the harsh light of noon and the fervent glare of artifice:
from the cruel nature of the out-of-doors and from the transitory
human feelings that seem alien to that nature, pale beside it.

> In the pines the thrush is waking—
> Lo, yon orient hill in flames!
> Scores of true love knots are breaking
> At divorce which it proclaims.
> When the lamps are paled at morning,
> Heart quits heart and hand quits hand.
> Cold in that unlovely dawning,
> Loveless, rayless, joyless you shall stand!

The conclusion is hopeless. It is an assertion not of how beautiful
natural things appear but of how the world destroys love, denies
marriage, and isolates the human creature by denying human values.
Better a retreat to womb-like darkness than a choice between ir-
reconcilable lights: "Dusk the hall with yew!"

What begins as a sad rejection of one kind of Romantic faith ends,
then, with a sad recognition that human desires are incompatible
with the sense of reality in a daylight world. If the simple allegory
sometimes creaks in "The New Sirens," the symbolic and metaphorical structure holds more firm: the shadow in which the sirens
stand and their fitful lights, seen from a distance, are more distinct
than the sirens are; in this shadow and against that light we can
imagine the poet watching, musing, and not only hearing but commenting upon their voices.

There is, of course, something radically imperfect about the poem
as a whole: it fails to be clear and, because its dim allegorical figures
are inadequate to the emotion they seem to inspire, it fails of
dramatic point. "A mumble," Arnold calls it. Still, the idea of a
remarkable poem is here. The poet is perhaps too entirely in the

picture, too much the speaker, and too much involved with the sirens, attracted to the life of intense feeling they embody, to see them steadily. But, if so, his vision is in the process of clarification.

"The New Sirens" can fairly be called a soliloquy rather than an oracle or a true dramatic monologue because it is unmistakably a pouring-forth of somewhat confused and very personal feelings in words addressed to no particular person, words intended to issue in no action. If, on his own or any other evidence, Arnold could be taken as an even occasionally religious poet, "Stagirius" (or "Stagyrus") might be put into quite a different category; but the poem itself poses the question whether it is in fact a petition to a listener. Its liturgical form, with the refrain "Save, oh! save," might suggest a traditional meaning rather than the sense of some "calm soul of all things" for "Thou, who dost dwell alone." But the words describe a human soul who cannot see the eternal God nor come near Him in a temporal world of doubt "where all is double," "where love is half mistrust,/ Hungry, and barren, and sharp as the sea." Traditional form controls and strengthens the desperate plea, the repetition and refrain intensifying a rather general diction; and yet the poem is essentially an expression of need rather than an assertion of faith, and if it moves us—as, at a perhaps simple poetic level, it may—the effect is not strictly that of faithful entreaty.

> Let all words be mild,
> All strifes reconciled,
> All pains beguiled!
> Light bring no blindness,
> Knowledge no ruin,
> Fear no undoing!
> From the cradle to the grave,
>   Save, oh! save.

These lines, finally, have the sound of a charm; they echo some magical incantation rather than the Prayer Book.

Even more obviously reflective (almost in the manner of an ode) rather than direct is the address "To a Gipsy Child by the Sea-shore"; but here the setting and the subject are particular enough to give dramatic depth to the poem at least as great as, say, that in "Resignation" (with its jumble of narrative and oratory within the monologue). In fact, the "Gipsy Child" is more unified than "Resignation" because it is more strictly limited to a scene, and because its themes appear to emerge from an experience rather than to be conjoined with it. The lyric quality of the poem is touching, too, the movement sweetly solemn, because of a finely modulated pentameter line (rhyming abab). Altogether, the effect of this form, this setting and this subject—the child gazing seaward—is vaguely Wordsworthian; but Arnold has produced a version of Wordsworth which is also a criticism and a rejection of Wordsworth's view.[2] At the heart of the poem are neither childhood joy nor the noble bearing in calamity, but gloom and grief.

The poem begins with four rhetorical questions.

> Who taught this pleading to unpracticed eyes?
> Who hid such import in an infant's gloom?
> Who lent thee, child, this meditative guise?
> Who mass'd, round that slight brow, these clouds of doom?

The import of Arnold's child derives from gloom, not joy, for the clouds with which his infant brow is clothed are not now those of glory. He is not Wordsworth's priest, not teacher but taught. The meaning of his mood is hidden in him, his guise is lent, and he

2. Lionel Trilling observes that this poem keeps the form of Wordsworth's myth of joy but changes the content so that it becomes a myth of tragedy. See p. 95 of Trilling's *Matthew Arnold* (New York, 1939).

cannot, as the poet of the Immortality Ode can, lend beauty to the landscape; he is the object acted upon and not the creative spirit. And acted upon by whom or what we do not know; again, as in the sonnet on Emerson, the questions are not to be answered.

The ironic echoes of Wordsworth are everywhere in the poem, in the contrast between subject and setting as well as in specific phrases. While earth, ocean, and the very sea-birds "labour on," in quiet work, the child is idle in no rapturous "superfluity of joy" but dully meditating, "drugging pain with patience." Sometimes the echoes are so clear as to suggest pure imitation: in the fourth stanza, the young child's aversion to his mother's breast, if not his alienation from the earth and sea, seems to come directly from the Immortality Ode. But his vision is only "soul-searching," and, in the fifth stanza, his profound glooms rather than any vision in a more poetic sense "enhance and glorify this earth." Here and at the conclusion of the poem, it is not the assertion of an immortality more than human that seems beautiful but rather the tragic, or at least pathetic, comprehension of human mortality and pain. (And perhaps there is an immortality of sorts realized even in that comprehension, as in the art of Shakespeare; perhaps, but Arnold still vacillates: in 1869 he cancelled the first stanza of the "Gipsy Child" and rewrote the ending of the fifth.) The language may be largely Wordsworth's, but the tone is elegiac and it is unmistakably Arnold's.

The child is weary as though of battle, sadder than any exile or a lost angel, and the suggestion of the seventh stanza is that he has had no earthly home from which to be exiled and no spiritual home from which to wander. He is like the stoic in keeping "disdainful silence" and like the disillusioned "gray-hair'd king" in loving life a little, loathing it more. But he feels a pain to which the stoic is indifferent, and he anticipates a grief that he has not experienced, with

that visionary's mind which, before "the long night [of death],
whose stillness brooks no star," will have "fathom'd life too far,/
Have known too much—or else forgotten all." For it is the peculiar
quality of this child, apparently (Wordsworth was right in this)
that he intuits the truth. His intuition is either lost or fixed in despair
by the philosophy of age as he grows up, but it is never to be forgotten entirely, even though

> The Guide of our dark steps a triple veil
> Betwixt our senses and our sorrow keeps;
> Hath sown with cloudless passages the tale
> Of grief, and eased us with a thousand sleeps.

Now, in this thirteenth stanza, the poet begins to reflect on the
human condition in general. We shift our attention for the moment
from the child and his setting as Arnold indulges, so to speak, in an
aside. The theatrical device, more dangerous for him than pure
soliloquy, leads from a thirteenth stanza that is only metaphorically
jumbled (it is not an indefensible jumble) to a fourteenth that is
very much more problematic:

> Ah! not the nectarous poppy lovers use,
> Not daily labour's dull, Lethaean spring,
> Oblivion in lost angels can infuse
> Of the soil'd glory, and the trailing wing.

This is the stanza, one suspects, which a good many readers would
choose as the loveliest in the piece: it begins classically and ends with
a fine Romantic phrase, with the pathetic conjunction of angelic
glory and the soiled, the feeble, or the broken. One has to disapprove
of these lines, however, as a meaningless embroidery or, worse, as a
contradiction of the whole poem. If the remark about "lost angels"
is to be read as applying to the subject of the poem, then one must
cite the first and fourth stanzas against this view of him: so far from

his appearing as one whose glory is soiled by mortal sorrow (and it is difficult to see what very different sense "soil'd" could have here), it is precisely that sorrow which is his glory and is said to "glorify this earth." Furthermore, the seventh stanza, with its attention on the child himself, concludes that "no angel's sorrow [is] so forlorn" as his, presumably because the child is not angelic, was not born "in an alien planet." If, on the other hand, these later lines are taken as only a general observation on man's inability to forget mortal pain, there is no justification for comparing men with angels; it is mere sentimentalism to do so—the speaker enjoys rolling a magnificent phrase without being able to mean it, only for the sake of the emotional charge it carries—and the figure is, at best, of very vague relevance. These few bad lines mar an otherwise beautiful poem and they indicate the difference between Arnold's poetry of experience, with its usually firm metaphorical structure, definite (and often symbolic) setting and direct observation, and that phrase-making which his imagination sometimes redeems but which has too little firm intellectual support beneath it to remain consistent.

The last three stanzas are consistent with the rest and they conclude the prediction of the child's future, so that one longs to tighten the structure by omitting thirteen and fourteen and beginning fifteen with a *but:* even if the child grows up to lead a strenuous existence, with a "just sun" gilding his "storm-vext stream of life," even if he is blinded by that "blank sunshine" and loses his insight into the heart of darkness, still, the poet tells him,

> Once, ere the day decline, thou shalt discern,
> Oh once, ere night, in thy success, thy chain!
> Ere the long evening close, thou shalt return,
> And wear this majesty of grief again.

To the movement of the busy world a man may be contentedly chained, but the glory of man, that which enhances and glorifies the earth, is his intelligence of himself as a tragic figure doomed to the pain of incompleteness and of isolation in time; this is the sense at the heart of Arnold's elegy, that man expresses his humanity, and his majesty, only in his tragic vision. So, finally, "To a Gipsy Child By the Sea-Shore" is more than elegiac, it is a celebration of the dignity of suffering man. If there is an answer to the rhetorical questions posed at the beginning of the poem, it is only that the source of this child's dark vision is the source also of his glory.

The questions are not, however, answered in more specifically religious or philosophical terms, just as the *Thou* addressed in "Stagirius" is not defined. It is likely to be the asking of questions, rather than the answering, with which Arnold's most memorable soliloquies are concerned. At best, when he cheers himself philosophically in his dejection, it is with this thin "Consolation":

> Time, so complain'd of,
> Who to no one man
> Shows partiality,
> Brings round to all men
> Some undimm'd hours.

But the poet's attempt to give form to a more profound dejection —a profound dejection which is his own—and to find consolation in that personal form, is difficult. Arnold is sometimes inclined instead, in his "Switzerland" poems especially, to go beyond stoicism and endurance, to explain and preach, as it were, to his own despair. The poet's feverish blood is never subdued by tragic clarity in those melancholy love poems, or anti-love poems, that celebrate his ambiguous emotional attachment to a Frenchwoman named Marguerite.[3] In them, the general questions of how time-imprisoned man can be in harmony with the vast universe and of whether men can communicate truly with one another are specifically introduced into soliloquy. In fact, the ways in which such matters are talked out, the vaguely philosophical terms with which these lyrics are filled, seem somehow to be out of keeping with the story hinted at; we have to suspect that Arnold is indulging in attempts at therapy, comforting himself with dark generalizations on his own experience, rather than rendering experience in such a way as to discover its meanings. The slightly strained tone in which so many of these poems speak, the insistence on desire and the all but theatrical exaggeration of despair, may amount only to the rationalizing of mixed and uncertain feelings. The theme of the poems, nevertheless—the failure in this world of any sustained passion—is an idea that receives indirect expression in one of Arnold's finest works, "Tristram and Iseult"; and it is worthwhile observing the direct statements if only as a prelude to that success. Furthermore, one of the lyrics in this group of soliloquies has some of Arnold's saddest and best oracular lines.

Although they were not finally included by Arnold in his 1878 grouping of the "Switzerland" poems, the first two pieces which refer to Marguerite are "A Dream" and "A Memory Picture": the first and better one a fantasy, with Arnold's familiar "river of life" carrying him away from the pretty girl on the shore, beyond "burning plains" and cities to be received by the ultimate sea; the second, "A Memory Picture," another attempt to save some fragment of

3. A thorough treatment of these poems and of the problem of Marguerite is included among Baum's *Ten Studies*, pp. 58–84. "Arnold might have said of 'Switzerland' what Meredith said of 'Modern Love': 'A writer's verse is one of his methods of relieving himself of the burden within him'; and he might have quoted—*We are betrayed by what is false within.*" (Baum's comment, p. 77.)

experience from the ineluctable flow of days. "Ah, too true! Time's current strong/ Leaves us fixt to nothing long." With more or less of this exclamatory manner, with this sense of subjection to some isolating temporal power, and often in a related water imagery, the seven lyrics of "Switzerland" sketch the "Meeting," "Parting," and final "Farewell" of the speaker and the young woman, his sense of their inevitable isolation from each other (in two poems) and his mixed memories and speculations about her ten years later (on "The Terrace at Berne"). In "Meeting," he listens to "a God's tremendous voice" which counsels him to retire; whether or not it is, as Professor Baum suggests, mingled with "the paternal tones of Dr. Arnold's memory," this voice sounds again like the ventriloquist's, giving external authority to an "inner-directed" but unexamined motive or, more accurately, to a partial motive, to an urging which the speaker must heed but for the truth and goodness of which he takes no responsibility.[4] He is guided by "Powers." (The "God" of "To Marguerite—Continued," the "Letters of Ortis" lyric, is no more clearly defined than the source of these words or the object of prayer in "Stagirius"; but Arnold shifts easily from "a God" and "guiding powers" to "the eternal Father" with his "Farewell.") The voice of Marguerite herself exerts some attraction in "Parting," although it is drowned out by the sound of the wind rushing toward the mountains of solitude; and the half-hearted lover declares that he wants to clasp her but cannot, because "a sea rolls between us—/ Our different past." The meaning of this phrase is not explained, but if we take it as a reference to differing social backgrounds, we may be tempted to take Hugh Kingsmill's simple view of the priggish poet. And yet no single explanation of the failure of love—her

---

4. But Baum (*Ten Studies,* p. 62) does not go as far as W. H. Auden, whose poem on Arnold declares that the poet was destroyed by becoming the mouthpiece of this paternal voice.

looseness, his higher mission, even his dimly philosophical sense of
being isolated by nature—rings quite true.[5] Even the speaker's ad-
mission in "A Farewell" of his feminine indecision, echoing Arnold's words about being divided and incomplete, is much less than
an adequate reason for the failure.

In most of these poems the terms and the voices shift and the tone
is uncertain (it varies from self-pity to bravura), for the poet has
tried to do either too much, by moralizing on a difficult experience,
or too little, by not being quite clear about what his moral is. In
the two poems on "Isolation," however, especially the second and
more celebrated lyric, Arnold makes a straightforward pronouncement on the nature of love which is at least clear—clear, controlled,
imaginatively developed, and consistently bleak.

The more extreme and less imaginative statement of every person's isolation comes at the end of the first piece, after the soliloquist's somewhat embarrassing address to his own "lonely heart"
("Back to thy solitude again!"). According to this conclusion, the
world's lovers, like the proud man of "In Utrumque Paratus," have
only "dream'd" their felicity, for there is no communion of heart
with heart. The first lines of the second poem echo that assertion in
Arnoldian imagery:

> Yes! in the sea of life enisled,
> With echoing straits between us thrown,
> Dotting the shoreless watery wild,
> We mortal millions live *alone*.
> The islands feel the enclasping flow,
> And then their endless bounds they know.

This is Arnold's poetry of statement at its best. We may regret the

5. For the simple view, see the chapter on "Marguerite" in Kingsmill's
generally iconoclastic *Matthew Arnold* (London, 1928), pp. 58–79.

italics and exclamations, but the diction is never strained beyond its occasion and the direct assertion is consistent with its tone, a "longing like despair," instead of emerging in shrillness or mumbles. The poet's mixed feelings have been located, especially at the end of the poem, in imagery and language which, at least for a reader who knows much of Arnold, have ironic point. The irony lies in another answer given to that question asked at the beginning of the "Gipsy Child," the question implied by "Stagirius" and variously answered or evaded by the poems of "Switzerland."

> Who order'd, that their longing's fire
> Should be, as soon as kindled, cool'd?
> A God, a God their severance ruled!
> And bade betwixt their shores to be
> The unplumb'd, salt, estranging sea.

"A God," in this stanza, has to be from a Christian point of view an anti-God, opposed to all the usual personal associations and associated instead with the natural sea against the human land—the land that is explicitly identified with religion in "The Forsaken Merman."[6] And it is not only this inversion that suggests an almost shockingly ironic use of God's name. The implications of the imagery represent a reversal of other poetic and philosophical assumptions than Arnold's own: both Donne's Christian assumption that no man is an island and the Transcendentalists' assumption that the oceanic Being includes us all. The same "God" and perhaps the

6. There are other poems in which some such oceanic and inhumane deity appears: in "Human Life" the unknown Power is an isolating power, as it is in "Self-Deception" (a rather stronger preachment) and "The Lake." But Professor Culler points out that the sea in "Isolation," which is unlike those in Arnold's other poems in being called "salt," is not necessarily identical with them; and, furthermore, that these lines could be more than a metaphor if the lovers' severance results from her being a Roman Catholic and his being a religious liberal.

same estranging sea (if "different past" can be expanded to suggest so much more) have occurred in the earlier poems of the group, but the concentration on one kind of imagery—and thus on both the charm and the hopelessness of human desire, both the vastness and the bitterness of the sea-nature—give this allegory of despair more power, make it more disturbing, than any of the other poems.

More power than "Absence," in which Marguerite appears to be translated from a literal figure into a useful memory ("Upon Time's barren, stormy flow,/ Stay with me, Marguerite, still!") and more power than "The Terrace at Berne," although that last poem in the group includes a rather fine echoing of the lines on isolation, with an even less substantial image for the poor creature buffeted by the eternal "sea of life":

> Like driftwood spars, which meet and pass
> Upon the boundless ocean-plain,
> So on the sea of life, alas!
> Man meets man—meets, and quits again.

Frankly mixed feelings and implicit irony are just what one misses in poems like "Urania" ("Excuse") and "Euphrosyne" ("Indifference"), in which the would-be lover perhaps protests too much in defense of his lady ("She is not cold, though she seems so"), with a too self-conscious nobility ("Adieu! and say that one, at least,/ Was just to what he did not win"). Again, voicing a resignation more meek than moving, he asserts that love, for "the sons of men," is illusory. What Urania demands is not a son of man, certainly, but a demi-god; she asks that

> His eyes be like the starry lights—
> His voice like sounds of summer nights—
> In all his lovely mien let pierce
> The magic of the universe!

However ludicrous the lady's supposed desire for a superman from "a worthier race than ours," there is no evidence in the poem of any ironic reflection on her terms.

Much more appealing, although they are not very impressive poetically, are the love poems which apparently reflect Arnold's courtship of Frances Lucy Wightman: "Calais Sands" and the group known as "Faded Leaves."[7] At best, they are pleasant occasional pieces; they consist of the musings of the poet as he waits to view his "Queen" in "Calais Sands," his description of the painful feelings of love in "The River" (which can be read as a monologue), the expression of anxiety in "Parting" (again, the lover fears that time will blur the memory of love), the bittersweet memory (in spite of that fear) in "On the Rhine," and the address to his absent beloved in "Longing," a neatly if obviously constructed end-piece to the group. The emotions of the lover, in these poems, leave little room for reflections on man and nature. The most generalized piece of all, "Too Late," is another oracle within a group of soliloquies, and although it accepts the guiding powers ("Each on his own strict line we move,/ And some find death ere they find love") it seems also to imply that not all lovers are like islands or driftwood spars. In fact, it refers in a platonic image to "the twin soul which halves their own." At least, unlike "The Buried Life" and the parts of "Switzerland," these are love poems; they do not insist that the same heart beats in every human breast.

---

7. The case for this reasonable conjecture, that the poems of "Faded Leaves" refer to Miss Wightman, is convincingly summed up by Kenneth Allott in the *Times Literary Supplement* of March 28, 1958, p. 172. Professor Allott here prints the manuscript versions of "Separation" and "The River," the latter including six quatrains never before published which would seem very clearly to link that poem to the English rather than the Swiss love affair: the river is identified in the first quatrain of this version as "the broad bosom'd lordly Thames."

Arnold's genius is not, however, that of the love poet. Most of his more celebrated soliloquies are of course specifically elegiac. Such poems mourn both the deaths of faithful men and the death of the poet's own faith. For these elegies are intensely personal; in them, more fully than in the records of his moods and fancies as a lover, Arnold finds voice and occasion to embody his most intimate feelings of desire, uncertainty, and frustration. And yet in the best of his elegiac work there is more than personal frustration. If he cannot be converted to a time-transcending vision of a whole and timeless order, as a poet Arnold can achieve an imaginative vision that will momentarily fix and dignify the time.

"The Scholar-Gipsy," like some other English pastorals, is a complex fiction that introduces direct observation and contemporary ideas into the conventional setting: its diction suggests the convention—with shepherds and flocks and lists of flowers—but its metrical form is beautifully original.[8] It begins with the apparently familiar pastoral voice speaking to some Corydon or Daphnis (or perhaps, as Tinker and Lowry suggest, to Thyrsis, that is, to Clough) but it focusses attention on the figure of the wandering gipsy, a figure alien to pastoral. The poem is developed, somewhat as "Lycidas" is, by a series of addresses. There are three monologue-like stanzas filled with graceful description and spoken to the shepherd, followed by three stanzas of narrative—the condensed story of Glanvil's poor scholar, in the form, it seems, of soliloquy. In the rest of the poem, up to the final image of the Tyrian trader, the poet's voice is speaking as if to the scholar-gipsy himself. Even though the speaker falters in his conceit ("But what—I dream!") it is restated as he insists at last that the gipsy lives and can be so addressed. We

8. The prosodic and stylistic effects of this poem and of "Thyrsis" are examined by Baum in his study of "The Two Laments" (*Ten Studies*, pp. 107–13).

do not expect an answer to the speech, any more than we do to Lycidas when he invokes the water-nymphs and Camus, for once the literal setting has been established and the shepherd-auditor has slipped away, we must assume that this is another kind of soliloquy, not monologue. But the gipsy who exists in the poet's imagination exists also, through the power of that imagination, in ours, and for the time we may be willing to accept our soliloquist's crucial assertion, "we imagine thee exempt from age."

This device of narrative soliloquy followed by imagined address, a device at once dramatic and personal, and in keeping with the pastoral convention, allows Arnold to criticize the life of his time by using the gipsy for the purpose of contrast; it allows him, furthermore, to project his image of a timeless and impossible ideal. "The Scholar-Gipsy" gives voice again to Arnold's anxieties about an all-powerful single order of endless change in which, as in the "sea of life," men are divided and confused, are fragments of what they dimly conceive their true selves to be. It also gives voice to a fleeting pastoral vision of youth and integrity triumphant over change and division.

Not that the vision could be fixed as a firm reality; it *is* fleeting, it is imagined (and not in the highest sense of that verb) because Arnold still cannot reconcile a universe of becoming with a universe of being. Remaining in some way subject to time, the scholar-gipsy is not really out of time. The series of landscapes in which he is pictured is distinctly seasonal: the Hurst in spring, the Cumnor hills in summer (the Fyfield elm in May, Godstow Bridge in June, the pastures in April), in autumn Bagley Wood and a wooden bridge in the chill winter. After these descriptions, it can be true only in a special sense when the speaker cries, "No, no, thou hast not felt the lapse of hours!" The "change to change" of the seasons is very literally described, and the gipsy who battles with the snows must feel it even if he experiences no nerve-wracking changes of heart and mind. Indeed, the scholar-gipsy's virtue lies not only in his being single-minded but also in his being patient and passive: his "one aim, one business, one desire" is to wait for "the spark from heaven." Clearly, he is not in heaven and he does not have the spark. He has not "spent his fire," and this fire may be associated with the "dying spark of hope" nurtured by the intellectual leader of the nineteenth century (Goethe, or perhaps Arnold meant Tennyson); but hope and patience alone do not in the world of seasons triumph over time.

The special sense in which the wanderer keeps his "perennial youth" is of course the sense in which he is alive for the speaker, who courts disaster by putting his ideal into so literal a setting and, finally, by giving advice to his own image of the steadfast man. When he advises the gipsy to fly from contact with the modern world and "its sick hurry, its divided aims," to fly, specifically, from "our mental strife," he can mean only that his living ideal must not be brought too long or too fully under the influence of the skeptical, the intellectually over-sophisticated side of the Victorian mind; just as it is to be seen only fleetingly in the landscape, this vision of the whole man must not be allowed to fade and die in such a harsh light: "Plunge deeper in the bowering wood!" Finally, the often-debated image of the Tyrian merchant at the end of the poem represents another fleeting, and fleeing, figure. The last two stanzas, like the ending of "Sohrab and Rustum" or more obviously like that of "Tristram and Iseult," shift the scene and subject, by the use of Homeric simile, so as to seem irrelevant to the story. In fact, they are an indirect comment on the story, not only because, as E. K. Brown observes, both the trader and the gipsy are aloof from the noisy world, but because both are dim Romantic figures invented by the speaker in his musings (for Arnold's gipsy is not Glanvil's).

Or, to put it more boldly, both are images for the speaker's lost self, which he is mourning. Even though the poem ends with the scene of a beginning ("And on the beach undid his corded bales"), its subdued tone is clear; "The Scholar-Gipsy" is included among Arnold's elegiac poems because it celebrates an ideal which can live only in poetic moments, only in the imagination as it is stirred by longing. Within the real landscape of the seasons, against the background of modern life, "with its sick hurry, its divided aims," the poet's faith in human integrity which outlasts time and change—in, precisely, the human soul—is dead. Or it lives, if at all, in a lovely daydream.

"Thyrsis," which is called an elegy because its purported subject is the death of Arthur Hugh Clough, is no more melancholy in tone, and it ends, somewhat unconvincingly, with an attempt to rally the spirits: to "animate and ennoble" as "The Scholar-Gipsy" (so Arnold has confessed to Clough) quite fails to do. It is a serious question whether its initial theme of desolating time is finally offset by the image of the elm-tree that remains, for the poem is weighted with past participles of finality: *changed, gone, lost, flown, fail'd, dead.* But the tree might be enough to stand against these negations, if Arnold were not constrained to say too much about it; it might at the very least replace the gipsy as an attractive image of the dubious ideal.

For the most part, the diction of "Thyrsis" is fine, if self-consciously fine; not the heightened colloquial diction of "Dover Beach" (which could absorb no "alack" or "methinks"), it is nevertheless condensed and unusually solid. The speaking voice is that of a poet: for all the rhetorical addresses to Thyrsis and the final conjuring up of Thyrsis' own voice, this is unrelieved soliloquy. Arnold often begins poems weakly and he almost always ends them well, but in this soliloquy the opposite is true. Its tone is beautifully established in the first line, "How changed is here each spot man makes or fills." Nearly every word is specially significant: "changed," of course, the most crucial word of the poem; the "spot man makes" (the city, specifically Oxford) "or fills" (the land, specifically the valley of the Thames); even "here," for this is a poem about locality as it is a poem about time. It is in fact an attempt to make what is unchanged of a place prove something of timeless value: "Are ye too changed, ye hills?" the poet asks, and hopes for a negative answer. But "here" may suggest more than Oxford, may suggest the sublunar world, and this sense of its opening line haunts the whole poem.

Oxford is beautiful to the speaker, but not so fair as it has been. He returns to the old familiar landscape with a feeling of loss, of change in himself and change in it. He has lost more than Thyrsis; he has lost the time and place and certainty in which he and Thyrsis once lived. In Wordsworth's version of pastoral that loss is touching but not final; in Milton the loss and anxiety about early death are real, but so is the resurrection; and even in Shelley's "Adonais" the death and renewal of the seasons give promise of some constancy, some kind of triumph over death. But Thyrsis, in Arnold's eighth stanza, is conquered by time, and the seasonal return of flowers and birds appears here only by way of contrast. The figure of Orpheus, once associated with that of Christ, is as alien now to the English landscape as is the power of the Sicilian shepherd to revive dead Bion. In fact, it is no promise of eternal life for Thyrsis, in heaven or in oneness with Nature, that the wandering soliloquist seeks; he looks only for a proof of steadiness, of any steadiness, in a world of unending change. He wants to hold fast to a faith in the scholar-gipsy, whose life is identified with the life of the elm-tree—faith, that is, in the integrity of the ideal man, an integrity consisting in his single-purposed searching for the whole truth. Again the poet seems to be seeking evidence that it is possible to be a seeker. We imagine Arnold considering the terrible earnestness of several-minded Clough (his flute soon "learnt a stormy note/ Of men contention-tost"), Clough who might serve as the very type of the Victorian seeker: "Thou, too, O Thyrsis, on like quest wast bound." But finally, after giving voice to his sadness and his sense of loss; after remembering the dingle that is plowed land now, the youthful view of "mountain-tops where is the throne of truth" which has faded into adult knowledge of the world's "unbreachable" fort and a disillusioned longing for the repose of death; after his retreat from the hunters and his sudden view of the tree, the speaker is inspired to imagine the voice of Thyrsis whispering clear and hopeful, whispering, presumably, from the "southern country" of the immortals. Thyrsis becomes, like the scholar-gipsy and the tree, a projection of his wavering faith, sought but only glimpsed and heard in precious moments. It is not so much a recreated Clough who speaks at the end of the poem as another of Arnold's familiar voices, the oracular voice declaring "proof" that "the light we sought is shining still"—that a Truth exists for which the scholar may hopefully seek.

"Thyrsis," then, is Arnold's attempt to recall the certainty of his and Clough's student days that single-minded truth-seeking is worthwhile. But it is more than that, more than an attempt to revive the scholar-gipsy in his soul. The poem is genuinely elegiac because the lucid and simple faith in man's having access to truth is dead, as Clough is dead. The tree and the gipsy are at best fleeting and ambiguous encouragements, and although Thyrsis becomes one of Arnold's voices at the end, the note sounded in the speaker's own voice at the beginning, the note of sadness in the knowledge of change, sounds on through the finest passages of the elegy as a ground bass for the lyric celebrations of the tree and the message of hope. "How changed is here each spot man makes or fills!"

The power with which so much of "Thyrsis" is charged derives largely from its tension between an urgent desire and a melancholy fact; but the final effect is not so true and moving as that of "The Scholar-Gipsy," where the poet does not feel obliged to force a too simple resolution. In comparing the two, one has to prefer the beginning and middle of "Thyrsis" but the ending of "The Scholar-Gipsy."

More purely and simply elegiac in mood, less complex and less remarkable because they hardly pose this difficulty, are the memorial verses for Wordsworth, for Edward Quillinan, for the poet's brother William, and for Charlotte Brontë. In all of these the elegist's voice speaks sadly but not desperately, nor perhaps even very intensely. It is resigned to the loss of "Wordsworth's healing power" in a poem ("Memorial Verses") that is interesting at least as a record of Arnold's critical opinion.[9] The rattling and somewhat perfunctory stanzas "In Memory of Edward Quillinan" are perhaps more than resigned to death: "Alive, we would have changed his lot,/ We would not change it now." To be sure, in a much higher strain, his "Stanzas from Carnac" (a straight tetrameter quatrain happily replacing the "Quillinan" abab version of ballad stanza) suggest the poet's inability to reconcile himself to the scene and manner of his brother's death:

> Oh, could he once have reach'd this air
> Freshen'd by plunging tides, by showers!
> Have felt this breath he loved, of fair
> Cool northern fields, and grass, and flowers!

9. In their commentary (p. 220), Tinker and Lowry observe of "Memorial Verses" that "this elegy is the first of Arnold's poems, apart from his sonnets, to disclose his abilities as a literary critic." It would deserve much more attention in an account of Arnold's critical development than it is given here.

But that regret is all but dissolved in the companion-piece, "A Southern Night," which finally accepts an exotic southern location for the graves of William Arnold and his wife, those "spent ones of a work-day age":

> Mild o'er her grave, ye mountains, shine!
>  Gently by his, ye waters, glide!
> To that in you which is divine
>  They were allied.

This conclusion, relating man and nature in a familiar but now literal imagery, goes beyond the vaguely Tennysonian longing for death of the Quillinan elegy and of "Requiescat," with its weariness of heat and sound and its desire for peace. It may even imply the faith declared in some of Arnold's oracles and, again, in the epilogue to his prosaic "Haworth Churchyard." The epilogue, which Tinker and Lowry call "Hegelian," denies that the Brontës sleep peacefully in their graves, not because they were in fact (all but Anne) buried in a vault but because some continuation of life's energies is to be imagined in the hereafter.[10]

> Unquiet souls!
> —In the dark fermentation of earth,
> In the never idle workshop of nature,
> In the eternal movement,
> Ye shall find yourselves again!

That assertion is quite as positive and pleasant as the assurance of

10. See Tinker and Lowry, pp. 227–38, for the circumstances of the poem (and some evidence as to Arnold's feelings about Harriet Martineau, whose death he prematurely mourns in "Haworth Churchyard") as well as the poet's presumably original version of it.

peace in death which it denies. But when Arnold is so nobly positive his voice is likely again to sound hollow; his rhetoric exclaims, his diction becomes grandly vague. Even in "Rugby Chapel," which substitutes for elegiac gloom the memory of his father's attempts to animate and ennoble a "fainting dispirited race," the attempt to declare some faith in an after-life is in fact a question.

> O strong soul, by what shore
> Tarriest thou now? For that force,
> Surely, has not been left vain!
> Somewhere, surely, afar,
> In the sounding labour-house vast
> Of being, is practised that strength,
> Zealous, beneficent, firm!

If anything, this passage is less convincing than the after-thought of "Haworth Churchyard" which it so strikingly parallels. "Somewhere, surely" is neither very specific nor very assured.

The finest part of "Rugby Chapel" is that which precedes this passage, the first thirty-six lines, where no attempt is made at sober analysis or high inspiration. These lines evoke a setting dark and cold—"Coldly, sadly descends/ The autumn evening"—and they insist upon that setting with almost every adjective and adjectival noun: *dimness, cold, solemn, unlighted, austere, darkness, gloom, gloom.* Even though that last word recalls the radiant vigor of Thomas Arnold's person as it stood out against such darkening days, his "ray of buoyant cheerfulness" fails to destroy wholly the autumnal mood. And when, in a curious and suggestive shift of imagery, the father is seen as a mighty oak in whose shade (!) his children, now "unshaded," grew, the ambiguity of the speaker's language is well enough established. It is only as he goes on to reassure himself and us that his strange true tone goes false. The imagery now shifts from that of the labor-house to that of the "midmost Ocean" in which "most men eddy about," and at last to that of a pathway through gorges, rocks, and mountain heights. Arnold returns again and again, of course, to the conception of life as a sea in which human feelings are ebbings and flowings of the moment. But the imagery of heights and ascending motion is not so natural to him, and he always imagines the mountains of truth (or, as in "Shakespeare," of vision) as distant and cloudy. There is something unpoetically inspired in the voice that cries,

> We, we have chosen our path—
> Path to a clear-purposed goal,
> Path of advance!

—especially when the goal is by no means clear-purposed. Onward and upward to what? To what is the father leading his pilgrim? The poet asks that question explicitly, and instead of answering it replies, "A God/ Marshall'd them, gave them their goal." And the poem concludes, with un-Arnoldian fervor, "On, to the City of God." But we need hardly recall that the God of that city, as Augustine meant and as Thomas Arnold would mean that phrase, is not only *a* God, we need hardly go outside the poem itself to detect a thinness and uncertainty in the allegory and the diction of this tribute.

In "Heine's Grave" there is no attempt made at such tribute pure and simple. In fact, the poem is surprisingly unkind for an elegy: it is, altogether, less lyric mourning than literary criticism, and although the speaker's sense of temporal limitation, of mortality, runs through the verse, it finds its relevance at last more to the poet who utters this criticism than to its object in the Montmartre tomb.

That was Heine! and we,
Myriads who live, who have lived,
What are we all but a mood,
A single mood of the life
Of the Spirit in whom we exist,
Who alone is all things in one?

. . .

O thou, one of whose moods,
Bitter and strange, was the life
Of Heine—his strange, alas,
His bitter life!—may a life
Other and milder be mine!
May'st thou a mood more serene,
Happier, have utter'd in mine!
May'st thou the rapture of peace
Deep have embreathed at its core;
Made it a ray of thy thought,
Made it a beat of thy joy!

Even Arnold's intermittent transcendentalism, of this sort, does not dissolve the hesitating self-consciousness of his most personal voice. This rhetorical question and exclamatory hope sound more genuine, perhaps, than the pep-talking of "Rugby Chapel"; but, having achieved much less of an elegiac note at the beginning, "Heine's Grave" comes to an only somewhat less dubious conclusion, with its prayer to be "a ray of thy thought,/ . . . a beat of thy joy!" Not so weak at its weakest, it is nothing like so sure at its best as "Rugby Chapel."

The "Stanzas from the Grande Chartreuse" do not offer this difficulty of the forced inspirational ending, for, although the poem is more complex than Arnold's public memorials, like those to

Wordsworth and Miss Brontë, it arrives at no stated resolution to a stated conflict. Indeed, the terms of its conflict are given so variously that it is difficult to grasp the thing as a coherent whole.[11] What the various oppositions have in common—between the monks' faith and "the world," between Romantic "nobleness of grief" and the same world's contempt for melancholy, and finally between the shyness of children secluded in a forest abbey and either the action of troops or the pleasure of hunters—is only an impression of peace and gloom set against one of mundane liveliness and light. The speaker's heart goes out to the gloomy settings, but not entirely: like a Greek in an alien land, a wanderer, he is not of one world or the other, neither worshipper nor scoffer, neither Romantic nor man of action. Even the long final image of the children who, like the poet of "Thyrsis," shrink from the noisy bands of troops and hunters, even this rather charming passage suggests something less than a commitment: "the poet" here, as Professor Baum says, "is neither for the Carthusians nor for the children." He is simply not "for" anyone or any side. This refusal of commitment is what accounts for the most poignant lines in the work. But uncertainty even about what he is alienated from and where, so to speak, the center of his conflicting emotions is located, accounts also for some confusion in the total effect.

If the poem were shorter, as short as "Dover Beach," it might have to be a good deal better—or if it had a setting which could compel the speaker, as the monastery does not, to confine himself to its symbolic possibilities, and if the soliloquy were thus dramati-

11. So Paull Baum points out in one of his *Ten Studies,* pp. 114–21. It is difficult, however, to agree with Baum that the poet's melancholy, when he feels himself to be lost "between two worlds," "seems to have nothing to do with his loss of orthodox faith or with his aspirations toward the star of Truth" (p. 117). The melancholy has to do at least with his lack of any single source of value to which he can either hold or aspire.

cally sustained. The principle of development mostly followed in this fairly long piece is that of association, association too little controlled and unified by either external objects (such as the Berkshire landscape) or internal consistency of idea. In this tendency to rather free association Arnold demonstrates the danger to his art of using the long soliloquy. The diffuseness of "The Grande Chartreuse" as soliloquy seems especially unfortunate because the poem has good things in it: those celebrated lines about "two worlds, one dead,/ The other powerless to be born," the stanza beginning "Our fathers water'd with their tears/ The sea of time whereon we sail," and the last seven stanzas. But as the rhetoric of the speaker changes its object of address—from the teachers of his youth to the monks, the "World," Obermann, and so on—and as the children's voices obtrude upon his own, the poem comes to seem not only inconclusive but, for all its beauties, fragmentary.

The "Stanzas in Memory of the Author of 'Obermann'" are like those from the Grande Chartreuse in presenting an almost kaleidoscopic shifting of images and a succession of melancholy reflections upon the times and the World. The all but saving difference lies in the speaker's now keeping his Alpine setting fairly well in our minds from the beginning to the end of the poem. Even so, the mountain setting is as usual misty, and the too familiar imagery of shipwreck, of shore and stormy ocean, fail to lend much vitality to his recital of equally familiar themes: "He only lives with the world's life,/ Who hath renounced his own," and

> We, in some unknown Power's employ,
> Move on a rigorous line;
> Can neither, when we will, enjoy,
> Nor, when we will, resign.

So, in spite of his returning finally to the scene of his soliloquy, the impression left by the speaker is not so much a specific and dramatic sense of grasping the person and the personal voice as it is a sense of being instructed, of having heard (not overheard) a series of more or less interesting critical and "philosophical" observations loosely strung together. (More loosely strung, in fact, than those of the later poem on Sénancour.) Because these observations are fairly flat, with little of the humanly mixed quality of the *cri de coeur,* the stanzas have not after all, in spite of their consistency of setting, the fine sad note we hear sometimes in the sometimes too tearful self-pitying "Grande Chartreuse." The interest we can take in this lament for Obermann and modern man is an interest in its ideas only; the best stanza here is simply the most concise summing up of an important idea:

> Ah! two desires toss about
> The poet's feverish blood.
> One drives him to the world without,
> And one to solitude.

Life on the mountain, solitude, quiet work in natural surroundings, the attempt to transcend the times if not time itself, these are the elements in Arnold's poetic vision of the poet's wholeness. They are not a means of escaping pain, for the poet must feel the pain and passion his clear and steady vision comprehends, according to several passages in Arnold, including the lines of "Philomela," ending with "Eternal passion!/ Eternal pain!" But the way of the poet would be unlike that of the gipsy wanderer in the world, imprisoned in time and seeking his soul not in art but in faith. Arnold's soliloquies suggest these several attitudes toward what he conceives of as the human dilemma; and they are likely, in either case, to sound tentative and melancholy, filled as they are with a brooding on the triumphs of time.

The poet's brooding on this subject is in effect a questioning of any fixed value in the universe of flux. In "Youth's Agitations" he asks how he will feel "When I shall be divorced, some ten years hence/ From this poor present self which I am now," and his answer is that he will be discontented, for the very "ebb and flow" of passions that now pain him and the "hurrying fever" will seem good to the older man who lacks them. What this poem indicates and Arnold elsewhere only implies is a skepticism about the reality of the human soul: if I am another self entirely in the future I am defined by circumstance and not by a real core of essence which is me. On the other hand, in "Bacchanalia, or The New Age" (a little more than "ten years hence"), Arnold denies the reality of progress—he is no more committed to that than he is to the conservative values—as one epoch succeeds another: there is only change in the world, there is no fulfillment. The poet has to know this, to understand what past and present have in common.

> The world but feels the present's spell,
> The poet feels the past as well;
> Whatever men have done, might do,
> Whatever thought, might think it too.

But the poet does not, apparently, see more than past and present; now, at least, there is no suggestion of a vision that sees either beyond or into time.

There are, of course, other moods and other views. The poet of "Thyrsis" and "The Scholar-Gipsy" can still at moments hope for the vision, for the faith in a human destiny, as he does once more in his rather oracular poem "Palladium," where the image for human identity is like the signal tree, an emblem standing now above the waters of change:

> Still doth the soul, from its lone fastness high,
> Upon our life a ruling effluence send.
> And when it fails, fight as we will, we die;
> And while it lasts, we cannot wholly end.

While it stands, "the battle in the plain" (about which, in "Dover Beach" and elsewhere, Arnold is to have mixed and mostly negative emotions) will continue.

But the less affirmative of these poems are the more personal and the more likely to have the sound of soliloquy. For Arnold, the advantage of the poetic soliloquy is that it allows him to give voice to such personal and passing attitudes, to speak his mind and mood without insisting on a positive message, even when his mind and mood are uncertain and unhappy—even when the sense of his own subjection to the tyranny of time is most compelling, most melancholy.

# 4. Monologue and Dialogue

ARNOLD'S FINAL classification of his verse includes a category of "dramatic poems" comprising only two works, "Merope" and "Empedocles on Etna." But there are other poems into which the use of setting and of *personae* enters significantly enough to justify their being termed dramatic and to justify our calling Arnold a dramatic poet. He cannot, however, be called a poetic dramatist, and the distinction is crucial for an understanding of his poetic power and of his limitations.

In fact, some few of his poems which are technically monologues sound rather like dressed-up oracles: the audience and situation, that is, appear to have little genuine effect in qualifying what the speaker says. It is only when Arnold produces a dramatic situation, a tension and even a conflict between two attitudes, or between the speaker's attitude and the reaction of his listener or the quality of the setting, that he is able to give objective and quite successful form to the inner dialogue, the "dialogue of the mind with itself" (as Arnold puts it in the 1853 preface) which oracular verse cannot fairly represent. Certainly there is no strong sense of dialogue achieved when the poet gives superficially dramatic form, the form of dialogue, to the utterances of his "Epilogue to Lessing's Laocoön." In effect, he refuses to recognize the limits to which quotation marks can be stretched. This piece of verse criticism was, to be sure, published after Arnold's period of poetic activity, in 1867 (all the other complete poems considered in this chapter appeared between 1849 and 1853). But even as criticism or as philosophy it lacks any justification for its fictive form: it has no such give-and-take as Dryden allows in his "Essay of Dramatic Poesy" and no Platonic accretion of ideas by dialectic means, for Arnold is neither a critic who appeals to general rules nor a philosopher who works by contrasts and alternatives. Interesting for its idea of the bardic function—which is to produce a vision of the moving "stream of life" and thus, implicitly, to criticize lives that diverge from the grand tendency of the whole—interesting because it suggests how sharply Arnold must have felt his failure to be a poetic visionary and an oracle, and perhaps, too, because it illuminates his use of the river and ocean imagery, the poem is altogether too much like a lesson to embody that "charm which Homer, Shakespeare teach." Maybe the first speaker deserves what he gets for asserting that there is more great painting and music than great poetry, and that poetry fails to "soothe our pains" as music does, but the well-bred *I* of the poem does not precisely contradict these assertions or the pragmatic grounds on which they are unfirmly based; and he does lecture at length and ponderously to his poor long-suffering friend. Again, Arnold is not at his poetic best speaking as an oracle, a lecturer, or prophet.

According to the aesthetics of this epilogue to Lessing, a true poet does more than record some "outer semblance," as the painter must, more even than the musician's work of communicating emotions; or, at least, a few inspired bards do more, for they reveal the scope and movement of life:

> They speak! The happiness divine
> They feel, runs o'er in every line;
> Its spell is round them like a shower—
> It gives them pathos, gives them power.

But Arnold's own finest poetry has almost none of this "happiness divine." When he forgets his duty to ennoble or inspire, or, in a serious sense, to charm, he imagines a "stream of life" that is as devious as the meandering Oxus of "Sohrab and Rustum," moving from uncertain sources to a mysterious ocean through a course that no vision, neither bard's nor prophet's, can explain. And when that imagination is dramatized, in either monologue or dialogue, the *I* who speaks is not the self-conscious bard—not, in the words of E. D. H. Johnson, the public man of letters—but a more vivid *persona*.[1] In place of the bardic *I* are Mycerinus, the merman, the sick King of Bokhara, Tristram, the strayed reveller—and even, sententious as he can be, Empedocles, who will not speak with more fervent assurance than he honestly can.

Somewhere between the amateur aesthetician of the "Epilogue" and the sometimes imperfectly projected Empedocles stands the speaker of "Resignation": his is a voice speaking in a landscape, a voice which can be good when it is not too garrulous, and when it is addressed to someone else in the landscape. This speaker, again, is concerned with the question of what a poet must be and do. He is concerned also with the subject that Arnold worries most often in his soliloquies, the subject of time, and with the question of man's place in the temporal order. Because it makes more use of indirection, of dramatic structure, and even a narrative line of sorts, the poem can for all its talkiness deal more clearly than, for instance,

1. Johnson's *Alien Vision of Victorian Poetry* contrasts the role of the man of letters with that of the artist; see especially the section in that book on Arnold, pp. 147–213.

"The New Sirens," with these abstract matters. It evokes a very palpable world in which, as well as on which, the speaker can make his observations.

The observations sound, once more, profoundly sad, and sadder at the end than the title might imply. Although this poem is one of the most readable statements of Arnold's intermittent Stoicism, touched here as elsewhere by something of the religious self-negation taught in the *Bhagavad-Gita,* the conclusion suggests a failure to attain either the philosophical resignation of the Greek or the self-forgetfulness of the Indian. Addressed to "Fausta" (in fact, to the poet's sister, the "K" of his letters), it could also in a sense be addressed by the poet to himself. The poem is written in tetrameter couplets that might lend themselves to the trenchant phrase, but it begins rather with a vision—a vision of men moving through time toward their "self-ordain'd" goals: pilgrims bound for Mecca, crusaders for the holy land, conquering Goths for Rome. These are men enthralled, in the sense of being enslaved, by their labors. They must always be moving; for them it would be pain unbearable "to thread back and to renew/ Past straits and currents long steer'd through." This metaphor of flowing water, introduced at the end of the first passage, is to occur again. But first the poet turns to his Fausta and speaks directly to her and specifically about attitudes toward time. Serene souls, he says, those freed from passion and struggle and resigned to the human lot, are unlike pilgrims for whom the hours must serve as handmaids; instead, they are the servants and pay "obedience to the passing day." And Fausta herself, who is obsessed, like Faust, with the temporal limitations placed upon human life— the phrase "Time's chafing prisoner" recalls the prison imagery in the first scenes of Goethe's masterpiece—is urged to be more like such resigned souls, like those who find freedom from conflict in accepting their roles as prisoners of time.

In the second part of the poem the scene is literal and present. The speaker and Fausta are retracing a walk they took with a party of friends ten years before, and the experience of renewing "past straits," of returning to that scene, with what appear to be even the same clouds and shadows (each thing is not changed *here*), is a pleasant rather than a painful one. As if to echo the metaphor of the backward-moving water, their movements are described in the figure of a flowing tide. A literal brook as well is in the scene: a brook that these two remembered having followed years before, for hours, until at last they "bathed [their] hands with speechless glee,/ That night, in the wide-glimmering sea." The poet remembers, too, the band of gipsies they met in this valley, and he muses on their roamings: although they are touched by time, the gipsies "rub through" with no more pilgrim zeal than philosophy. And, being a poet, gazing on a scene apparently untouched by time, he muses further on the artist's proper view of temporal things. At this point in the poem the transitions are a little difficult, but one must follow the speaker's mind as it wanders, in a psychological rather than a logical movement. The movement is in fact more progressive than it appears to be, and not so nearly personal and arbitrary as the development of Arnold's soliloquy in "The Grande Chartreuse." The speaker's mind is focussed—and the objects in the landscape as well as his memories are brought into that focus—upon the brevity and pain of human life. The question he implies is the question of how to use one's time.[2] He supposes that if the gipsies enjoy freedom from anxiety and struggle it is because they are so close to cyclical nature and so little absorbed with past and future. If the poet can, with more difficulty, extricate himself from bondage to transient ends it is because he sees not so little but so much, because he hears

2. This is precisely the concern of Arnold's other poem addressed "to Fausta," and entitled "A Question."

"the murmur of a thousand years." Recreating history, he can achieve a vision of beauty without desiring it, and he can experience isolation without suffering loneliness, can be at one with the world and yet apart from it.

> Before him he sees life unroll,
> A placid and continuous whole—
> That general life, which does not cease,
> Whose secret is not joy, but peace;
> That life, whose dumb wish is not miss'd
> If birth proceeds, if things subsist;
> The life of plants, and stones, and rain,
> The life he craves—if not in vain
> Fate gave, what chance shall not control,
> His sad lucidity of soul.

In these lines which so neatly parallel the crucial passage of the later "Epilogue," "happiness divine" has not yet replaced "sad lucidity." Again, using two typical and recurrent figures in his poetry, Arnold compares and contrasts the sad way of the poet, the visionary, with that of the gipsy wanderer. They are two ways of escaping from anxieties about time, by rising wholly above the moment and by sinking wholly into the moment. And again, as in "Quiet Work," the "general life" which the poet imagines in viewing the whole world of apparent time and change is essentially placid, silent; it is essentially the life of inanimate things, not the life of time-conscious, which is to say self-conscious, man. This is a hard view for ordinary men to take. As Fausta smiles, the speaker imagines her thinking that gipsies and poets are the one less, the other more than most men, that she is still what she was, a prisoner "in the day's life, whose iron round/ Hems us all in," and that hers is "the common life of men." This common life of men, certainly, is not the general

life of things which the poet's vision reveals; and the poet's only
answer to her supposed objection is that she may cease being Fausta,
may transcend the experience of the common in the vision of the
general by first resigning herself to the iron round. Now his voice
is almost an echo of Krishna's speaking to Arjuna in the *Baghavad-
Gita*. Almost but not quite, for it lacks consistency and it falters at
the end.

What the Hindu scripture reveals is a nature in some sense above
as well as within the phenomenal. But, clear and pragmatic as his
knowledge and conclusions are, knowing "love transient, power an
unreal show" in a world that outlasts all human feelings, and knowing man can escape pain only by freeing himself from these feelings,
Arnold has no clear enough compensating vision, no sublime form
to give the human needs with which he must in final honesty deal.
As he turns from the values ordinary people have in common he
imagines other men who,

> To men's business not too near,
> Through clouds of individual strife
> Draw homeward to the general life,

and one thinks perhaps of the saintly Emerson; but it is difficult to
feel much enthusiasm for saints of negation unless that phrase refers
to a real home and is not a bit of mere rhetoric. When he assures
Fausta of their wisdom

> in His eye,
> To whom each moment in its race,
> Crowd as we will its neutral space,
> Is but a quiet watershed
> Whence, equally, the seas of life and death are fed,

one must wonder who He is, to have an eye. Not, certainly, the

God of Jews and Christians, who is a God in history and for whom each moment, far from being neutral, is filled with moral and sacramental meaning, is unique and irreclaimable. We have to suspect again that Arnold has only used a manner of speaking, and that the manner, showing up his indistinct version of an Eastern religion in the language of a Western religion, is fatal to his message.

The last section of the poem, as if Arnold now felt the failure, is neither transcendental nor resigned but earth-bound and melancholy. The image of a watershed, echoing the metaphor of life as a stream and the memory of the brook's flowing into a sea with which relief and joy were associated, has made both human life and any other movement toward fulfilment in time seem meaningless. Now, the "stream that falls incessantly," along with other phenomena, appears "to bear rather than rejoice": there is no ultimate ocean to be hoped for. The tone of these last lines—"Enough, we live!"— is less Hindu or Emersonian than Stoic, and it is not at all perfectly Stoic. As he sets the general against the individual and common, the poet still takes the view of a man living in time and feeling its inadequacy; rather than objectifying himself, he gives human feelings to the objects of nature. He ends by being not so much resigned as disillusioned:

> Not milder is the general lot
> Because our spirits have forgot,
> In action's dizzying eddy whirl'd,
> The something that infects the world.

Neither Stoicism nor the higher view can finally alter the scene, as the speaker retains his orthodox sense of a real earth and of real death in it (without the orthodox faith that does not give itself to nor transcend this earthly nature but trusts to raise it).

The poet's message to his Fausta, written some time after "Resignation" ("Resign nothing that you have in deference to me or my oracles") confesses that the urgent voice of faith is thin, is liable to falter. But when his oracle is dark or when the dramatic framework controls his poetry, the result is less urgent and less faltering; the facts of life as Arnold imagines them speak loudly enough.

In "Mycerinus," a poem more than half of which is monologue, addressed by a king to his people, they are grim facts. Mycerinus, the young king, must recognize the prison of circumstance in which he is bound, and he is clear about the injustice of his fate—so virtuous a ruler, to die so young, while his father "loved injustice and lived long." The king is isolated from his fellows by this realization that the gods do not observe the human rules of justice. Disillusioned, he determines to imitate and even compete with the careless deities by giving up his last remaining years to forest revels, or so he seems to do. He retires into a grove where, like Arnold's sirens, he turns the very night into artificial day.

> When the sun went down,
> A hundred lamps beam'd in the tranquil gloom,
> From tree to tree all through the twinkling grove.

But still he lives with his thoughts, he has not forgotten what the gipsy child so early learns. "It may be," the poet puts it, that the figure of death, like that of the slave in "The World and The Quietist," speaks to him as he lifts his bowl. And it may be that he gains an ennobling control, a stoical or Epicurean command of his feelings, in these years, taking "measure of his soul," knowing its strength. But, whatever may be, he has retired from the world of daylight, from the human community, to a womb-like other place that is rather like those dark halls of the sirens, artificially lit; and, at the same time, like the scholar-gipsy, he achieves a steadiness of life which ignores the changing seasons, weather, night and day.

So six long years he revell'd, night and day.
And when the mirth wax'd loudest, with dull sound
Sometimes from the grove's centre echoes came,
To tell his wondering people of their king;
In the still night, across the steaming flats,
Mix'd with the murmur of the moving Nile.

These appealing lines may amount to a fantasy of escape from day-to-day life with its dimming memory of the past and sharpening anxiety about the future. And yet the meaning of the conclusion is not perfectly clear, for we vaguely recall that a voice may have spoken to Mycerinus. Arnold has not been able to resist that hopeful possibility which qualifies and makes indefinite his ending. About the tone of his monologue to the people we are sure, but we may not be cettain whether the young king ends his days in steadfastness, with inner strength, or as a self-indulgent Romantic and a reveller who never strays.

In "Mycerinus" and in other more or less dramatic poems Arnold still (and always) finds it difficult to accept the dark picture that his imagination has to draw from his ideas, for he still combines a Christian moral temper that gives peculiar value to man and to human time with his insistent post-Romantic notion of "Nature" as a whole in itself that makes both time and man trivial. When he imagines the natural world as a setting for human actions he finds the human situation almost unbearably desperate. He cannot escape his Christian feelings: they qualify every response and indirectly provide the grounds for criticizing the Stoic or the pantheist or the materialist idea. This means that, like Tennyson and unlike Browning, Arnold finds human isolation the subject of his best dramatic poetry and a profound, even despairing, melancholy its mood. Because his thinking leads him not to resignation but toward despair, he is tempted to hedge—to hint, for instance, that a voice may yet resolve the dilemma—but he knows that, when his vision is whole and his own voice true, the vision will be of suffering, even if the poet must suffer in imagining it.

So it is in "The Forsaken Merman," a poem that is not interrupted by ambiguous voices or, like "Resignation," devoted explicitly to philosophical questions. This clearly and consistently fine monologue is all the more striking a commentary on the relationship between man and nature, artifice and impulse, for being wholly dramatic and indirect. With "The Forsaken Merman," the internal conflicts which make so much of Arnold's work seem fragmentary become a source of poetic tension, and the problems take symbolic form.

In the sonnet written in Butler's sermons and in the most memorable of the poems to Marguerite, man is pictured as an island surrounded by isolating waters; in "The Gipsy Child" he is pictured at the edge of land, gloomily looking seaward, as the poet pictures himself in "Dover Beach." Standing now at the same edge but seeing with the eyes of the other side is the sea creature which represents all that is attractive in non-human nature. The element of water, symbolic "Mediator between the inanimate and man," as Arnold is to call it, is the mother and home of this man who is less —or more—than man, to whom the land is forever alien. The water world that always fascinates Arnold appears, in "The Forsaken Merman," as the natural world of flux and freedom; the conflict between it and the human land is associated now with the conflict between the isolated natural self and the social or moral self, as the theme is once more introduced of the brevity and the frustration of human love.

The monologue has an irregular rhythm, with subtly irregular rhyme, suggesting at once the movement of wave upon wave and the echoing sound of a sea voice.

> Come, dear children, let us away;
> Down and away below!
> Now my brothers call from the bay,
> Now the great winds shoreward blow,
> Now the salt tides seaward flow;
> Now the wild white horses play,
> Champ and chafe and toss in the spray.
> Children dear, let us away!
> This way, this way!

The merman and his children call to his human mate their mother (whose name Margaret suggests that of the lost beloved in the "Marguerite" poems), but she remains in the "white-wall'd town," with its "little grey church on the windy shore." We may notice that the sea wall and the church are the most prominent features of this town; and that, bathed as they are in sunlight, they lack the color, the green, red, gold and amber, of the underwater places. There is, furthermore, a pointed contrast between stillness and dim light in the caves of the sea, and the sounds of bells and music and the light of the sun that belong to the civilized land.

> Children dear, was it yesterday
> We heard the sweet bells over the bay?
> In the caverns where we lay,
> Through the surf and through the swell,
> The far-off sound of a silver bell?
> Sand-strewn caverns, cool and deep,
> Where the winds are all asleep;

> Where the spent lights quiver and gleam,
> Where the salt weed sways in the stream,
> Where the sea-beasts, ranged all round,
> Feed in the ooze of their pasture-ground;
> Where the sea-snakes coil and twine,
> Dry their mail and bask in the brine;
> Where great whales come sailing by,
> Sail and sail, with unshut eye,
> Round the world for ever and aye?
> When did music come this way?
> Children dear, was it yesterday?

The bells and the music are associated with the church: on the dry land of human society the distinctive human force which holds society together is religion. The wall holds back the sea; the church calls men together, it is the heart of the town. In order to return to the church, to unite with her kind in common prayer, Margaret has left her sea home. These elements are in the Danish ballad which is Arnold's source for the story, but he has added to them, first, by taking the merman's rather than a landsman's point of view, second, by intensifying the contrast between dry sunny land and the deep dark ocean caverns with their beautiful beasts and sea-snakes, and, finally, although it may seem a minor point, by making the season Easter.[3]

> Children dear, was it yesterday
> (Call yet once) that she went away?

3. In George Borrow's version the day is only "a festival morning." For Borrow's translation of the Danish ballad (in which the wife is named Agnes) and this re-telling of the story (where she is called Grethe), either or both of which may have been Arnold's source for his poem, see Tinker and Lowry, pp. 129–32.

Once she sate with you and me,
On a red gold throne in the heart of the sea,
And the youngest sate on her knee.
She comb'd its bright hair, and she tended it well,
When down swung the sound of a far-off bell.
She sigh'd, she look'd up through the clear green sea;
She said: 'I must go, for my kinsfolk pray
In the little grey church on the shore to-day.
'Twill be Easter-time in the world—ah me!
And I lose my poor soul, Merman! here with thee.'

Of all times, Easter is the most joyous for the orthodox, and of all Christian festivals it is the most peculiarly Christian. One may with a liberal mind celebrate the birth of a divinely inspired leader or even his martyr's death; but at Easter the Christian chuch declares that a man who was dead rose again, in the body, at a particular time and was manifest as God. It is at this time of resurrection, the most radically unnatural event, that Margaret rises from the grave-like, womb-like caverns of the sea and returns from natural to human life. But hers is no single-minded triumph over a nature that rejoices with her rising. If she has gained her soul, which she was in danger of losing with the merman, she has lost her love, her natural delights: in a certain sense she has had to lose her life in order to find it. This is Easter from the point of view of the depths.

When the merman and the children gaze into the church, they must stand on gravestones, objects unknown to their kind. It is to physical mortality and the hope of unnatural life that Margaret has returned, from natural immortality and the spiritual death which is peace. And this mortal hope is, for Arnold's merman, embodied in human noise, in the sounds of the Easter mass from which he is excluded: "Loud prays the priest; shut stands the door." From priest and holy book, from the alien town, he must turn back sadly to his own world in the knowledge that Margaret's choice is for her, too, a sad as much as a joyous one.[4]

> Down, down, down!
> Down to the depths of the sea!
> She sits at her wheel in the humming town,
> Singing most joyfully.
> Hark what she sings: 'O joy, O joy,
> For the humming street, and the child with its toy!
> For the priest, and the bell, and the holy well;
> For the wheel where I spun,
> And the blessed light of the sun!'
> And so she sings her fill,
> Singing most joyfully,
> Till the spindle drops from her hand,
> And the whizzing wheel stands still.
> She steals to the window, and looks at the sand,
> And over the sand at the sea;
> And her eyes are set in a stare;
> And anon there breaks a sigh,
> And anon there drops a tear,
> From a sorrow-clouded eye,
> And a heart sorrow-laden,
> A long, long sigh;
> For the cold strange eyes of the little Mermaiden
> And the gleam of her golden hair.

As a beloved, as a sexual object, as a mother, Margaret belongs to

---

4. The point is not the same in Arnold's "The Neckan," where the sea creature can, apparently, be saved in spite of the priest, so that he is lonely at last, but not in a religious sense lost.

the seascape of nature; only in the civilized pursuits of work and worship is she other than natural. The conflict between a natural and a social life, then, is expressed both in the symbolic contrast of sea and land and in her behavior. Neither of the alternatives is complete in itself; for the social, the civilized man must feel himself incomplete and so must the natural man:

> She will hear the winds howling,
> Will hear the waves roar.
> We shall see, while above us
> The waves roar and whirl,
> A ceiling of amber,
> A pavement of pearl.
> Singing: 'Here came a mortal,
> But faithless was she!
> And alone dwell for ever
> The kings of the sea.'

The merman is alone, but so, he remembers, is his cruel Margaret. On the land, companionship results from communion, from common worship: men are brothers when they have one Father, marriages are made in the image of the divine spirit's marriage with the flesh. In the ocean, kinship derives from immanent bonds, the bonds of the family which are those of living flesh alone. But either way without the other is imperfect. The woman and the merman both long for an impossible perfect union of the moral way and the way of the animal, without which Easter is, after all, incomplete and the sea is lonely.

Arnold does imaginatively join the two, even as he reveals them in conflict. His Margaret can live at the bottom of the sea and his merman can feel human love and sadness: only their environments keep them apart. For the poem is about the conflict between two ideas in one mind as much as it is about the isolation of persons divided by an "estranging sea," persons whose ways of life are incompatible. Both woman and merman can be taken as images of man—or, if one is concerned with intellectual biography, as Arnold's conflicting images of himself, or parts of a personality longing to be whole.

The longing and deep sadness of a divided man are given poetic form, dramatic form, in the voice of the merman. The natural sympathy which subtends "Quiet Work," the vague discontent with an attractive life of animal passion about which "The New Sirens" speaks, the mood of dissatisfaction with a world of mortal things in which transitory man is caught, the mood of "Resignation," are all involved in this poem; so that here, as in no reflective fragment, the mind and imagination of one who seeks for wholeness find a poise, a momentary wholeness which is not something more than was dreamt of but is very much more than has been achieved in his philosophy.

Another instance of this wholeness is Arnold's most celebrated lyric, "Dover Beach." As Murray Krieger has shown, the speaker in this monologue is carried beyond his temporary vision of the peaceful waters, by the ocean sounds, to a sense of eternal conflict between sea and land—the conflict embodied in the merman's speech.[5] We might observe, too, that the implications of the sea as an image are exploited in three ways, by the last three verse paragraphs of "Dover Beach." First, it is an image of constant change (the ocean is, in this sense, time, which destroys the steadfastness of men):

5. " 'Dover Beach' and the Tragic Sense of Eternal Recurrence," *University of Kansas City Review*, 23 (Oct., 1956), pp. 73–9. As the end of this paragraph indicates, I must differ with Professor Krieger on his use of the word *tragic* in the interpretation of Arnold's vision. But his close explication of the poem is sensitive and valuable.

> Sophocles long ago
> Heard it on the Aegean, and it brought
> Into his mind the turbid ebb and flow
> Of human misery.

✳ Second, it is an image of vitality, associated with the waters of birth and of baptism:

> The Sea of Faith
> Was once, too, at the full, and round earth's shore
> Lay like the folds of a bright girdle furl'd.

❊ Third, it is an image of blankness, formlessness, and mystery:

> for the world, which seems
> To lie before us like a land of dreams,
> So various, so beautiful, so new,
> Hath really neither joy, nor love, nor light,
> Nor certitude, nor peace, nor help for pain.

All of these are "natural" characteristics, but the sea has now become more complex and shifting in its meanings than it was even in "The Forsaken Merman": now, religion itself is conceived of not as a dry-land phenomenon but as a withdrawing tide. And whereas two of these interpretations derive from the past—"long ago" and "once"—the third is a realization about the present; for the whole world of nature comes at last to replace a specific sea in one time and place. This nature only *seems* to be the land of dreams that religion by sea-change would make of the dry land, and really has nothing to offer which the faith would read into it (no joy, no love, no light, no certain truth, and no peace and help). In fact, although "the world that lies before us" would seem, from the vantage point of the window established in the first verse paragraph, literally to be the ocean, that world is viewed as naked now so that this literal ocean is no longer, in a profound imaginative sense, sea-like at all; it no longer connotes even the ebb and flow of emotions tragically realized. (As Arnold complains in "The Grande Chartreuse," the "sea of time" is not watered by human tears in our day, the human situation is not dignified by a sense of the tragic.) The symbolic setting of the poem, including the bay, is transformed at last not into a third version of the sea, with its associations of changefulness and vitality, but into the scene—and this is a modern image for "the world"—of a darkling plain filled with confusion, ignorance, struggle, darkness. Such a vision is terrifying, but not in the fullest sense of the word tragic, for it denies moral grandeur to man in his temporal struggles. Apparently it even denies any relevance to the present of an image which always suggests, to Arnold especially, the mysterious and vital whole of nature.

If this interpretation is justified, if the speaker in "Dover Beach" can fairly be supposed to remember and reject several poetic ways of viewing the scene before him, finally turning from the attractive setting of the waters to the less lovely but truer symbolic equivalent for his disillusioned mood, the dark dry land, then that progression of thoughts to which he gives voice and which this sort of explication makes seem orderly and oracular is, one must add, neither so apparent nor so simply theoretical. The poem is saved from dull simplicity by the existence of a literal setting as well as a metaphor, of a speaking voice and a spoken to, a "love," as well as an idea. "Dover Beach" includes elements from several of Arnold's various kinds of poetry: it is consciously dealing with general, even philosophical, questions, like the sonnets, and it involves speculations very much like those that appear in the soliloquies. But, from the last line in the first descriptive passage, we cannot forget it is a monologue, and at the end the voice of the monologue is not the pure bardic voice. It is, rather, the voice of a lover disillusioned by the world, a thoughtful man standing with his beloved at a window overlooking the bay. Even the colloquial effect of the relatively free rhythm (up to the firmer, more formal last paragraph) reminds us of that fact. So, as he proceeds by association from the literal image of the first section through the larger tragic and religious metaphors of the second and third to the largest image of all, the "darkling plain," moving from the wholly literal to the wholly metaphorical, from small to large abstractions (misery, faith, the world) and from past to present, this logic of the speaker's mind is less apparent to us than the unifying mood.

More even than a general criticism of the modern world, "Dover Beach" is the poignant expression of the desperate need for love which men feel in this world, devoid of a grand conception of itself. It can be read as a commentary on the loneliness of modern man haunted by the fear that he may be isolated first from the universe and then from other men, and so cease to exist as a man. In the plea, "Ah, love, let us be true to one another," almost every word bears special weight: as the meanings of the ocean shift and blur, the poet's faltering faith in an oceanic whole—the dim belief that man can sink to the depths of himself and live as the waters do, that "the same heart beats in every human breast"—is destroyed; love becomes a fact, even a person; and the adjective "true" is opposed not only to the idea of infidelity but to the verb "seems." There is a negative echo, then, of "In Utrumque Paratus" and "A Summer Night" in these lines. But the most significant contrast to those poems lies not in the denial of a transcendental "land of dreams" so much as in the fact that the voice of "Dover Beach" speaks *to* a person rather than *of* mankind, and speaks to a person who does not only seem but truly exists. *You, I, we, us,* the pronouns of the poem give specific and dramatic reality to the common situation.

"Dover Beach," "The Forsaken Merman," and the other poems of Arnold's that embody a common humanity in this specific way are, like the soliloquies, poems of sorrow; for sorrow, even if it lacks tragic heightening, appears to him as that which is common to all men. For that reason, Shakespeare's brow gives speech to pains, to weakness and grief. And so "The Sick King in Bokhara" dramatizes the link between a poor criminal and his monarch-judge, both subject to laws of time and of space, of abstract justice and of inbred nature, which work to their suffering. The royal speaker in this dialogue shares the sense of subjection felt by a man who, having cursed his mother in a feverish moment, begs to be punished by death according to the legal code. That demand reveals something more than the guilt of Browning's Ned Bratts, for it involves so slight an infraction of the law; even if the literalism of it seems distorted from the point of view of a morality that considers motive and circumstance, the demand implies a deep psychological need alien to such sophistication. What Arnold's source, Sir Alexander Burnes, would consider the act of a bigot or a madman, might also be called a profoundly human if guilty and irrational compulsion.[6] The King not only recognizes this compulsion but, against his Vizier's advice, asserts his brotherhood as a fellow-subject with the "dead dog" by carrying his body to the grave, washing, and burying it. The pattern of this poem is tighter than that of the comparable "Mycerinus," the rhythm less colloquial, so that the figures speak and move as it were with formal gestures; but, marred as it is here and there by excessive stateliness, the dialogue between King and Vizier achieves a certain substantial quality in giving voice

6. For the source, and for Burnes's view, see Tinker and Lowry, p. 88.

to Arnold's vision of sick men in a land of drouth, subjected to both inner and outer compulsions which it is their dignity (a dignity almost tragic) to recognize and accept.

Even in Arnold's most dramatic moments, his characters are more likely to accept and suffer than to act. It is not surprising, then, that when he tells the story of Tristram and Iseult, he chooses to dramatize the lovers' last hours; nor that, with the combination of dialogue and narrative he makes of the story, he produces one of his few altogether beautiful long poems—a poem, again, of passivity, of dark recognition if not of acceptance.

This first modern treatment of the dramatic tale, which is also Arnold's most genuinely dramatic poem, betrays, it must be confessed, some characteristic weaknesses: an occasional failure of the poet's ear, the vatic urge that intrudes now and then to spell matters out too plainly, here and there a slightly coy or sentimental turn to the diction. Nevertheless, it is a completed work, the rather cool tone of which is remarkably consistent, a work that beautifully sustains the elegiac mood. The loss of passion, the moral and emotional fatigue about which Arnold elsewhere says so much, he embodies here. As Lionel Trilling observes in commenting on his letters to Clough, Arnold knows "that the poet does not express ideas but rather makes objects which by their shape and texture . . . are ultimately meaningful"; "Tristram and Iseult" is another one of the poems in which that knowledge bears its golden fruit.[7] The ultimate meaning of this poem is that the fragile intensity of human passions is soon dimmed and destroyed by time.

The objects imagined in the poem—the colors, the human and artificial figures, the landscapes invested with emotional significance —carry this sense quite as much as the elements of the Tristram

7. See Trilling's introduction to *The Portable Matthew Arnold* (New York, 1949), pp. 17–18. The words are, of course, a paraphrase of Arnold's own.

story that Arnold took from La Villemarqué, Dunlop, and Malory.[8] These objects are arranged in patterns of contrast, of light and dark, heat and cold, land and sea, which, along with the brilliant use of colors, give the sensuous correlative for idea and emotion: for the urge toward death and that toward life, for passion and the denial of passion.

We might, briefly, look at some of these objective means used in the poem: at the colors, settings, and then the metrical effects. *Pale, blanch'd, white* are the adjectives applied repeatedly to each of the three main characters, for whom the three sections are entitled. In the first part, although there are touches of gold in the picture of the pale knight and others—the gold of his harp as well as that of the ornaments worn by the two Iseults—the only light comes from a dying fire and a ghostly moon; and when Iseult of Ireland comes, she appears to Tristram as a ghost. The details of gold and green— the harp and the mantle cast over the knight's feet—are reminders of Tristram's green and gold youth as "hunter, harper, knight." They burst into light only in his memory of the "sweet green fields of Wales," of Iseult's "green Isle," of the "gilded barge" and the "golden cup": images from the spring-time of love. Tristram's feverish memory is colored by the bloody red of battle, too, which comes to be associated with the fever in his blood, his frustrated passion that neither the outcome of battle nor the "solitudes of the green wood" have availed wholly to calm. The only other place in this section where bright visions occur is the last passage, the picture of Tristram's golden-haired children asleep in their room, a passage which, like the last third of the poem, may seem irrelevant to the familiar story but which is, like that and some others of Ar-

8. See Tinker and Lowry, pp. 106–24, for these sources, and for a discussion of the poet's conception of the story as well as the variant passages included in the Yale manuscript version of the poem.

nold's strangely appropriate endings, a commentary on the whole. For the children dream, through their father's dying hour, dreams that are fairer than the literal sight of "wet red leaves . . . jewell'd with bright drops of rain" and the "glittering sea" in moonlight. The brilliant colors are again dream-like and distant; and however sentimental the description of these children with their "angel heads," it is clear that their dreams are fleeting—as is the vision of Tristram, who sees "fairer in [his] dreams" of the dead past than in the dying present. Imagination, youth, and energy are associated with gold, green, and red, with colors which, in "The Forsaken Merman," belong to the fantastic life of the sea; and the fleeting colors of passion, of fever, pain and desire, enter this scene only by way of dreams, of memory and fantasy. Black, white, and grey define the literal setting for this picture of pale mortality.

Even in fleeting moments the bright hues evoke an ambivalent reaction. The color in Iseult's cheek that surprises King Mark's courtiers is the brightness of disease, of fever; and for her as for Tristram this fever of desire is a restless baffled longing. The whiteness and the darkness of the second part—the flickering candle and the blanched sheet, the dark room and the raven hair—suggest for the lovers a release from longing, the release of peace, of coldness, of death. At the end of this section, the "ghostlike tapestry" flaps in the wind and the green-clad huntsman on it appears to be alive, while the cold knight, unmoved, "seems of marble on a tomb." The paradoxical transformation of the image into a live man and of the man into an image emphasizes once more the paleness of the dead Tristram, and it helps to give a monumental dignity to that paleness, that stillness.

But the colors of the third and final section, "Iseult of Brittany," with its landscape in the sunshine as it is seen by the children, are bright in fact and not only in memory. Heather and grass, scarlet

berries and glittering hollies bring into the present a vision of youth
and of verdant nature. And the story told in this last part, of Merlin's
enchantment by Vivian, takes place in "a green sea of leaf and
bough," a place like the greenwoods of which Tristram dreams.
For all the touches of gold and scarlet, the dominating color of the
poem is finally green. The contrast is between childhood, youth,
passion in the greenwood, and age, weariness, coldness, in the dim
light or dark. What occurs at the end, however, is the invasion of
one world by the other: the mood of weariness enters into the
greenwood in the story Iseult of Brittany tells her children. For
Iseult and the Vivian she describes come to assume the poet's apparent view of passion, the views of lines 111 to 150, that passage of
direct comment (which Arnold wisely omitted in the editions of
1853 and 1854) on joy that cannot be sustained in "the gradual
furnace of the world" or under the impact of some "tyrannous"
single thought: "How this fool passion gulls men potently." The
cold Vivian represents a natural loss of feeling and the eager Merlin
an unnatural, but very human, slavery to it. In fact, although the
oracular passage (re-inserted in the edition of 1857 and kept there-
after) makes a very good summing-up of Arnold's most melancholy
view, relevant certainly to his "Switzerland" poems, it is likely to
strike us as an encumbrance on the poem, since the remarkably
beautiful ending of the whole ("for she was passing weary of his
love") shows fully what the comment tries to tell.

And, as a conclusion to this poem with all its shifting cadences
and its evocations of dark and colorful objects, the story of Merlin
and Vivian does much more than illustrate an idea about the brevity
of normal human love. The elements of the strange forest and the
enchanted sleep reminds us of other parts of the poem and import
special significance into this story. It was in a "drear forest" that
Tristram's dying mother bore him; in the "solitudes of the green-

wood," wandering, he saw his vision of Iseult; and he fancies, as he dies, that she and he have lived "in the greenwood, all our lives, alone." The hunter on the arras, too, stands in "a fresh forest scene," until he seems to come from his "free greenwood" into the knight's chamber, asking, "What, has some glamour made me sleep"?—like Merlin aroused. The forest and its green are associated with birth and death, passion and enchantment, love and loneliness, and there is always something at once mysteriously dark and vital about the setting. It is as if the greenwood were at once a womb and a grave, and as if the poet's art, through something like Vivian's glamour, could fix the living man in its "plot of magic ground" as a fantastic means of escape from both the tyranny of passion and the shutting up of eye and ear, by fusing the images of womb and grave, by symbolically joining potential desire and ultimate peace. Imagination can make the hunter on the tapestry come to life, and it can change life into the beautiful death of art: it can transform landscapes into the fairer vision of dreams; dying lovers into marble statues; or doting Merlin into a sleeping immortal ("prisoner till the judgment-day"). Each of the three parts of the poem ends with such a transformation. The last, especially, is a transformation effected by the poet's highest powers, imaginative and prosodic.

The variations in meter and rhyme scheme in "Tristram and Iseult" are quite interesting and, except when Arnold tries to sustain tetrameter couplets in the first part, remarkably successful. Even the syncopated abab sections of dialogue between the lovers at the beginning of Part II are curiously appropriate, giving a distance and, as it were, a flatness to their speeches:

> Raise the light, my page! that I may see her.—
> Thou art come at last, then, haughty Queen!
> Long I've waited, long I've fought my fever;
> Late thou comest, cruel thou hast been.

The four-line stanzas are spoken alternately until first Iseult and then Tristram makes a longer speech (still in this form), and then at last, in four theatrical lines that sound almost like a duet, they join voices to form the unit. Tristram is speaking:

> Now to sail the seas of death I leave thee—
> One last kiss upon the living shore!
> *Iseult*
> Tristram!—Tristram!—stay—receive me with thee!
> Iseult leaves thee, Tristram! never more.

In contrast with the very artificial sound of these lines, the narrative continues:

> You see them clear—the moon shines bright.
> Slow, slow and softly, where she stood,
> She sinks upon the ground;

and so on. The lovers in their dialogue seem to be playing roles (virtually operatic roles) whereas the narrative and descriptive lines, closer to the rhythm of speech, reveal them more objectively and more movingly. Arnold's *liebestod* does not end with Iseult's passionate "never more" but with another sound:

> For these thou seest are unmov'd;
> Cold, cold as those who lived and loved
> A thousand years ago.

And so the whole poem ends, on an elegiac note—modulated, however, at last, by a sense not only of weariness but of peace in the magic circle of the greenwood. The grand simplicity of Arnold's final couplets gives to his imaginative retirement from the grounds of human strife and passion something of the elegiac beauty of other last lines; particularly the ending of "The Scholar-Gipsy" with its picture of withdrawal and that of "Sohrab and Rustum" with its image of consummation in death.

> They sate them down together, and a sleep
> Fell upon Merlin, more like death, so deep.
> Her finger on her lips, then Vivian rose,
> And from her brown-lock'd head the wimple throws,
> And takes it in her hand, and waves it over
> The blossom'd thorn-tree and her sleeping lover.
> Nine times she waved the fluttering wimple round,
> And made a little plot of magic ground.
> And in that daisied circle, as men say,
> Is Merlin prisoner till the judgment day;
> But she herself whither she will can rove—
> For she was passing weary of his love.

This conclusion of "Tristram and Iseult" is one of what Tinker and Lowry call Arnold's "tableau endings."[9] All is still, after the display of passion frustrated and passion suffered. In the tale told by young Iseult, the mood, once more, is that of sad recognition: there is no resolution, either intellectual or dramatic, for the conflicts embodied in the earlier dialogue, but only the beautiful fixing of a melancholy experience. According to the doctrine of the Preface of 1853, in which Arnold explains his withdrawing of "Empedocles," that is not enough; but there is one work, a poetic rather than an explicitly critical document, in which Arnold seems to defend this kind of poetry (and to ignore the demand that poetry inspirit and rejoice). This statement in the form of dialogue is "The Strayed

---

9. They include in their list of poems that end with such tableaux, "Mycerinus," "The Grande Chartreuse," "Thyrsis," "Dover Beach," and "Rugby Chapel," as well as "Tristram" (in the commentary, pp. 213–14).

Reveller," in which an inspired young poet gives voice to a sense
of suffering as the very substance of poetic truth.

In the series of vivid scenes which this young man of vision describes to Ulysses, the man of action, we have the impression of
human life in all its variety. First, as the gods watch it,

> They see the Centaurs
> In the upper glens
> Of Pelion, in the streams,
> Where red-berried ashes fringe
> The clear-brown shallow pools,
> With streaming flanks, and heads
> Rear'd proudly, snuffing
> The mountain wind—

and, with a more broken rhythm now, with a series of energetic
verbs, as the bards feel it,

> They see the Centaurs
> On Pelion;—then they feel,
> They too, the maddening wine
> Swell their large veins to bursting; in wild pain
> They feel the biting spears
> Of the grim Lapithae, and Theseus, drive
> Drive crashing through their bones; they feel
> High on a jutting rock in the red stream
> Alcmena's dreadful son
> Ply his bow.

Drinking of Circe's cup, the inspired youth can see the landscape,
faun and maenad "without pain, without labour." But the bard, it
seems, unless in such rare moments of intoxication, is neither an objective viewer of things nor a moralist but a man who communi-

cates his vision of the world by involving himself imaginatively in
what he sees:

> such a price
> The Gods exact for song:
> To become what we sing.[10]

This conception of the poet's business can be contrasted with the
one implicit in "The World and The Quietist," a much slighter
piece, in which Arnold defends his "debating" in "mournful
rhymes": his is one of the "adverse voices" that fall upon the world's
ear; he is like a white-robed slave who speaks to a great king in the
midst of his feast. Speaks what word? we wonder. But the poet is
once more vague when we most wish for a specific answer. Even
the title of the poem is baffling. It is difficult to see why the poet or
the slave is a quietist in any strict sense of that word, that is, a religious mystic; and, to use Arnold's own imagery, the poem has to
do with voices that speak out in the midst of the world's activity,
not at all with worldly noise and poetic quiet. Nevertheless, "The
World and The Quietist" may be regarded as an apology for one
kind of verse, including most of Arnold's sonnets, and "The Strayed
Reveller" as the statement of another extreme view. Poems like
"Resignation" and perhaps "The New Sirens" are in some inter-
mediate category, involving the poet's direct comment upon his life
and his times but a comment given allegorical or dramatic form.
"Mycerinus," "The Sick King in Bokhara," and "Tristram and
Iseult," where attention is directed to the aspect and action of persons
far removed from the viewer in time, place, or situation, represent

10. Lionel Trilling makes an interesting analysis of this passage, referring
to George Mead on the Romantic "assumption of roles," in his *Matthew
Arnold,* pp. 98–9.

the vision of the strayed reveller who has wandered from the worldly feast into the temple of a god, and who sees wide, like the poet of "Resignation," but feels deeply as well: feels frustration, pain, and loneliness.

We have remarked, now, a number of theories in Arnold's verse and prose as to the poet's proper function: the theories of "Resignation" and the "Epilogue to Lessing's Laocoön," which emphasize the controlling vision of a larger whole within and beyond the various movements of life; the critical and oracular theory that adds prophecy to vision; the more purely inspirational (as in the 1853 preface); and what might be called the empathic theory of "The Strayed Reveller." But, interestingly, this last view, the one which could be taken to give the firmest ground for dramatic poetry, is expressed by Arnold in negative terms: it is not joy, not action which the poet imagines and communicates but sadness, suffering. The theory of "The Strayed Reveller" is true to Arnold's practice, as much of his critical theorizing is not. And both the practice and theory, while they produce a poetry that is dramatic in the limited sense of giving voice to characters in contrast and under tension, are unable to produce a wholly dramatic structure. Arnold cannot be a playwright.[11] At the same time, so conscious of his poetic difficulties that he must again and again construct these theories and defenses of poetry in his poetry, Arnold is usually at his poetic best when he

---

11. The lack in mid-Victorian literature of a serious theatrical work, the weakness of Tennyson as a playwright, Browning's channeling of his dramatic talents into non-theatrical forms, all of these facts suggest that there may also be more general reasons for Arnold's failure to be a dramatist. He himself argues, in a note included among the Yale manuscript papers, that a writer's mature occupation with ideas about man and society must distract him from the observing and representing of others that is the work of a dramatic poet. This statement would not hold true for all poets or all times, clearly, but it does seem to apply to the Victorians.

is more like a playwright and less like an aesthetician or a moralist.
In his soliloquy he can embody the uncertainties of one man's
thought and speech; in true monologue he can begin to dramatize
the complexities of his own imagination; or in dialogue these complexities can be displayed—if not worked out in action—against a
setting that contributes further to the communicating of the anoma-
lies, the conflicts of experience.

Arnold fails to be very effective as a prophet in his verse because
he cannot successfully test any dogma against his imagination; his
imagination is too critical. He fails to be a playwright, perhaps because he cannot ignore the problem of faith, the challenge of intellectual order and wholeness. He cannot find an ending for events
—either a happy ending or a properly tragic one, or, even, a totally
negative and disillusioned ending. Genuine conflicts are beautifully
recognized in Arnold's best poetry; they are not resolved.

Nevertheless, he is devoted to the tragic muse (as he is to the
tragic Rachel); he tries his hand at several imitations of the Greek
chorus, and it is perhaps inevitable that he should once attempt what
he cannot quite achieve. *Merope,* the attempt at a Greek tragedy in
English, although it includes some fine blank verse (along with
some lapses into an almost spasmodic exclamatory style), never succeeds in establishing any true conflict or question to which the final
action can provide a denouement. "And all this by the Will of the
Gods," the final chorus concludes; in spite of the debate between
Merope and her son Aepytus over the proper method of opposing
the tyrant Polyphontes, and in spite of Merope's finally mixed feelings about the usurper—who is morally ambiguous enough to have
been an interesting character if we saw or heard more of him—it
all seems too easy. The gods are with us all the way. To be sure,
Aepytus is no brooding, suffering figure: he acts, and the outcome
of his violent action is happy. And yet there is neither dramatic

tension implicit in his acting, because no strong enough force opposes his urgent motive, nor tragic exultation in its result, because the object of his revenge, Polyphontes, has not been fully enough realized to make his downfall rouse either pity or awe. There are other reasons for the failure of *Merope* as a play: its blurring of dramatic focus, for instance, and its simply melodramatic elements, as in the unintentionally comic scene when Merope almost kills Aepytus with an axe. But these faults have been dwelt upon enough, and perhaps too much. It is not, in fact, so bad a poem as it has sometimes been called: its development, if neither very dramatic nor very tragic, has some interest of its own, and some of the choruses, like the one that reflects the dangerous misunderstanding and reconciliation of mother and son in the story retold of Callisto and Arcas, are worth knowing. The failure of the work to be what it sets out to be lies, after all, in the poet's inability to imagine an intensely felt discord of attitudes not only suffered but resolved by action. Even the most static of tragic protagonists acts, through his suffering, against terribly real forces, physical or psychological or moral. Arnold's Merope and Aepytus, although they were meant to appear on the stage as well as the page, are never called upon to be such actors.

If *Merope* fails because resolution is too easy, Arnold's other dramatic poem so-called, "Empedocles on Etna," fails to be a perfectly dramatized poem because resolution is impossible. Aepytus, with too little of his creator's sense for the conflicts in experience, can act; Empedocles, truer to Arnold's vision, can only suffer and die. But his sufferings and their setting are complex and difficult enough, and crucial enough for an understanding of Arnold's philosophical dialogue, to deserve close attention—the kind of attention given it by Walter Houghton, for example, who analyzes the poem carefully, indicating especially the distinction between Empedocles' more-or-less positive Stoicism, his thought, and, on the other hand, his largely negative feelings of ennui, his isolation from the society of his time, and his dissatisfaction with solitude.[12]

Several ways of looking at nature appear in the poem: the way of the physician, the way of the philosopher, and the way of the poet; of Pausanias, Empedocles, and Callicles. Arnold is too much a poet not to let the young harp-player have the first and last words, the words that are sung. In the meantime, however, there is a good deal of talking as well as a good deal of suffering.

The scene of the talking is a lonely mountain top, a setting that may recall the imagery of "Shakespeare" and "In Utrumque Paratus." To this height of isolation the exiled philosopher has come with his physician friend, followed at a distance by the musician Callicles, a strayed reveller from the feast below. It is the youth who first describes this scene in lovely detail and asks, "Apollo!/ What mortal could be sick or sorry here?" But he has hardly asked this question when he is joined by Pausanias, who tells him that he may play his harp but must remain out of the sight of the heart-sick and sorrowful Empedocles. After some talk about the philosopher's

12. See *Victorian Studies*, I (June, 1958), 311–36. This cogent analysis, indicating the emphasis on thought in Part I of the poem and on feeling in Part II, also makes a case for "Empedocles" as "the most impressive poem of its length written in the Victorian period." Although *impressive* is an adjective that the work might be said to invite, this is perhaps exaggerated praise. The "content" that Professor Houghton speaks of (p. 336) is in part a brand of Stoic thought which, even if it is "a view widely held today," will strike many readers as repellently cold. I must confess that it strikes me that way, so that the comments here may be distorted by lack of sympathy for Arnold's main character. But the poem has other modern admirers. Frank Kermode, who is interested in the isolation of the Romantic artist and of his symbolic art, which Arnold of course reflects, finds "Empedocles" not only a significant but "in some ways a great poem, profound and finely designed." See *Romantic Image* (London, 1957), p. 12 ff.

miraculous revival of a woman named Pantheia, a matter of some
professional interest to Pausanias, the singer retires, and Empedocles
appears, to listen and to speak.

As he first speaks, Empedocles appears to be somewhat insecure
in his moralizing. When he preaches reliance on the mind to Pausanias, his friend quotes the wise man's own words which he is now
understood to contradict: mind, he once said, is a mocking light
that leads men false who trust it. Apparently the self-conscious mind
vacillates between two diametrically opposed notions about itself.
We might almost suspect Arnold here of oblique self-criticism;
Empedocles may seem, like his creator, to be a bundle of contradictions. But the philosopher is spared having at once to resolve or
explain the contradictions; he is interrupted, as the poet sometimes
is, by a lyric strain, by the song of Callicles. The song is, first,
literally descriptive. It soon proceeds, however, to the description
of a mythical scene, the scene on Pelion where Achilles was taught
"all the widsom of his race" by the centaur Chiron. In striking contrast with the singing of Callicles is the philosopher's speaking: as
the music ceases, Empedocles, "accompanying himself in a solemn
manner on his harp," solemnly begins to intone a kind of monologue on the human situation. The learning of Chiron, of whom
Callicles has sung, was clear and definite; but not so the wisdom of
the moderns, according to this monologue. Empedocles' view of
man's environment is not the heroic view, for there are no real gods
in it, but only metaphors, and "the earth," "the world," "experience" are men's teachers, not the elders who communicate traditional lore. As for the human mind, or soul, it seems to be a mirror
hung on a cord in space, that "a thousand glimpses wins,/ And
never sees a whole." It cannot be surprising that one glimpse will
sometimes appear to contradict another:

The Gods laugh in their sleeve
To watch man doubt and fear,
Who knows not what to believe
Since he sees nothing clear,
And dares stamp nothing false where he finds nothing sure.

But Empedocles goes on to ask, "Is this Pausanias, so?"—and he adds "I will not judge." For he is concerned at the moment less with the metaphysical than with the pragmatic. What, then, is this modern man (Empedoclean or Arnoldian), this man made up apparently of bits and fragments, of momentary views if not of transient convictions, to do? How is he to believe and act? Empedocles' answer is a classical one, and it implies that the human mind is altogether something more than a mirror:

Once read thy breast right,
And thou hast done with fears!
Man gets no other light,
Search he a thousand years.
Sink in thyself! There ask what ails thee, at that shrine.

One can sympathize with Pausanias' confusion. Empedocles has abruptly and without explanation shifted from the tentative image of man as a dangling mirror to that of a profound human nature which is its own shrine; he is, again, stating two apparently contradictory views of man, one that leaves him isolated from the general nature of things and one that suggests his identity with that nature. The contrast, however, may not be a contradiction but only a distinction between man's illusory individual will and his "natural" self; this more-or-less Stoic distinction would be consistent with the advice Empedocles gives to Pausanias (and for him it may be good advice) to stop worrying about his destiny and settle with the world on modest terms.

For the reader of Arnold, Empedocles' wisdom is not wholly original. Man is born, he says, with the "thirst for bliss," but it is a thirst that cannot be quenched, for the world does not exist to make us happy. No, "born into life we are, and life must be our mould." The quiet world of things outlasts us, we come new into it and stay briefly in it; it is, moreover, indifferent to us: "streams will not curb their pride,/ The just man not to entomb," as Mycerinus knew. A man must, then, compose himself in the Stoic way instead of inventing such myths as God and Fate. But finally, what he finds within himself, the shrine to which he must sink, would appear to be an unself-conscious nature that is more—or less—than human, for Empedocles goes on to speak of man as being of one substance with outward things, in a vaguely pantheistic scheme that again recalls Emerson and the Hindu scriptures:

> All things the world which fill
> Of but one stuff are spun,
> That what we rail are still,
> With what we rail at, one;
> One with the o'erlabour'd Power that through the
>            breadth and length
>
> Of earth, and air, and sea,
> In men, and plants, and stones,
> Hath toil perpetually,
> And travails, pants, and moans;
> Fain would do all things well, but sometimes fails
>            in strength.

This rather unreliable Power seems not to include, for Empedocles, the moral qualities which Arnold sometimes wishes to find in it, for it is not to be personified either as an object for blame or as a hope for the redemption and raising of man and his world. Having, then, at some length, exposed the vain illusions of simple animal faith and of religion, and insisting that the thirst for bliss cannot be quenched, that the "longing of our youth/ Burns ever unconsum'd," Empedocles concludes with some commonsensical advice: live for the here and now, forget your dreams, and be content with present pleasures. We may feel, at the end of 350 lines of this solemn speech, not that this is such very bad advice but that it is more familiar than profound, that it need not be given in such portentous accents, and that it might better be put more briefly.

If the monologue is now and then sententious, however, it is beautifully complemented by the lyric of Callicles that follows it. The song tells of Cadmus and Harmonia, the aged couple who have been, after a life of pain and frustration, transformed into "two bright and agèd snakes" basking in the green Illyrian hills. In it the poet's art, drawing upon myth, imagines a human fate that is at last in harmony with the natural environment, a destiny not of resignation but of fulfillment, of thirst quenched and ardor stilled. In the eyes of Callicles there is always an ultimate relationship between the landscape, the gods, and men; for him, even when it is frightening, the landscape is particular, not allegorical, and it is in some way beautiful. The contrast between philosopher and poet is revealed in this way especially, as a contrast between two modes of seeing and feeling about man's surroundings. Arnold's wise man, when he imagines the mind as a mirror, is only repeating a familiar metaphor; to him, the mind is far from being "naturally," as Wordsworth puts it, "the mirror of the fairest and the most interesting properties of nature." And, for all his final insistence upon the ultimate oneness of his essential being with the natural elements, he is no longer able to find a human and very personal quality in the forms of nature. It is the philosopher's dignity that he is aware of this, aware of his own tendency toward an excessively dry and intellectual view that alientates him as much from his spontaneous self as from society. Only the poet, deluded or more than humanly perceptive in his celebration of a mythical harmony, has either the vision or the illusion of color, melody, and peaceful consummation in the world of elements.

And so Empedocles stands, at the beginning of the second act, alone

> On this charr'd, blacken'd, melancholy waste,
> Crown'd by the awful peak, Etna's great mouth,
> Round which the sullen vapor rolls.

Still, weary as he is and disillusioned, unable even to follow the prudent advice he has given to Pausanias, he turns, as if to his friends, to the elements which seem so grim. "Receive me," he says, "hide me, quench me, take me home." The word "quench" here has two meanings: both thirst and fire are quenched, the one satisfied and the other extinguished. And the satisfying of Empedocles' desire would, in fact, mean the extinguishing of his restless flame of thought. But again, in perfect contrast, the fire of the volcano is seen by Callicles as a vent of feeling, and, while the philosopher stands on the very brink of Etna, the musician sings of the rebel Typho buried beneath this mountain's roots, whose groans drown out all music and reach to the ears of Jove. In Callicles' song the roaring of the giant and ominous hues of the mountain are a part of beauty, for his art does with this melancholy waste what Empedocles' way of observing cannot: jets of flame and a lonely rock-strewn glen become, for the poet, animate and expressive; the groaning of pain and rebellion makes, for the gods, a harmony. To Empedocles these are combinations of the eternal elements, distinct in themselves and essentially without any mythic expressiveness. Whereas Callicles' song is mythopoetic, transforming the elements into human meaning, Empedocles inclines to transform man into an elemental state, to reduce mind to substance. He makes of the story about Typho a comment upon his alienation from society. He knows very well that the rumbling of the volcano is a natural phenomenon, but there is truth in this tale of the rebel titan, the truth that such a "brave impetuous heart" is likely to be crushed and oppressed by more cunning men.

As Empedocles discards his Apollonian laurel bough, Callicles sings again, and again the matter of his song is as terrible as the music is delicate. It is the story of Marsyas the faun, who is vanquished in a fluting contest by Apollo and, for his aspiring to rival the god, loses his life. Perhaps Empedocles finds in Apollo the image of his own virtually inhuman, and yet not god-like, state: he cannot live with other men and he can no longer bear to be alone, isolated both from human society and from the ultimate life of the elements. For, in spite of his appeal to those "friends," he is too fully aware of their nature to feel at one with them in this mortal life, or to celebrate the elemental world in myth as Callicles does. He may be tempted to find some sympathy in them—to imagine that the stars are melancholy survivors of a great world populated by the gods—but his clear mind will not let him, although, with a very Arnoldian use of pathetic fallacy, he sees courage and force in stars, sky, earth, and sea: "I alone," he cries, "Am dead to life and joy." So, like the poet of "In Utrumque Paratus," Empedocles finds solace in the metaphorical assigning of life and emotion to objects which are, from a human point of view, dead. The living can be dead to feeling; the dead elements are in some way alive. It is to death thought of as the life of the elements that Empedocles would give himself. And yet, even at the brink, he is tortured by the "devouring flame of thought." Can it be quenched and drowned in "our mother earth's miraculous womb," in the common life of the ultimate sea, in fire or air? Here, finally, in the imagery of the elements, what lies behind the myth of death and transformation, the story of death and resurrection, is stated: the question about man's relationship with nature, the question to which Arnold's imagination always tends:

> But mind, but thought—
> If these have been the master part of us—
> Where will *they* find their parent element?
> What will receive *them,* who will call them home?
> But we shall still be in them, and they in us,
> And we shall be the strangers of the world,
> And they will be our lords, as they are now;
> And keep us prisoners of our consciousness,
> And never let us clasp and feel the All
> But through their forms, and modes, and stifling veils.
> And we shall be unsatisfied as now;
> And we shall feel the agony of thirst,
> The ineffable longing for the life of life
> Baffled for ever.

If all desire is fruitless pain and if the conscious mind is an isolating and illusory principle, if the thoughts of men are false to their "only true, deep-buried selves," then there is fulfillment only in death, and maybe (terrible thought) not then. The first proposition alone amounts to the view of "The Gipsy Child," that the human being knows himself in knowing pain and suffering; but Empedocles goes farther, from a nearly tragic glorification of the mind to an almost total rejection of it. And at the very end he seems to believe after all that he can reject it, that he can sink into the general life and find atonement with the elements. He even uses religious language in the final instant. Indeed, Arnold's Empedocles has a nearly Christian sense not only of radical imperfection but of guilt—he thinks of the excessively intellectual self as causing man to be false to his true self —and his difficulty is perhaps more religious than philosophical, when he cannot find in treachery, cruelty, and despair, the necessary parts of a whole and therefore beautiful pattern, as Callicles does in singing of Marsyas. But, like almost every one of Arnold's sad and lonely characters, he is a monist, so that for him the sea of things will at best, in the highest moment of affirmation, seem to submerge mankind, if men cannot wholly transcend its elemental nature. In Empedocles Arnold displays a Stoic intelligence along with the critical imagination that can, at least, lead to the destruction of the Stoic—in an act which may be regarded as heroism, perhaps, or as the gesture of defeat.

His philosopher leaps into the crater shouting, "Receive me! Save me!," and his saviors are not God or man or God in man but the fire and the sea.

Whether the human mind is destructible, whether Empedocles' flame of thought and his agony of thirst are quenched, the final comment does not suggest. But these are the phrases one recalls from that last long extraordinary speech, rather than the momentary expression of faith in a philosophy; and it is life, beauty, Apollonian radiance, and order, that Callicles' last hymn celebrates, the permanence of life in unique and various forms, rather than their annihilation. Apollo is the patron, still, of medicine and the arts. By discarding his laurel, Empedocles has thrown off his allegiance to that god, but Callicles retains his, and his view of the elemental world still associates it with the gods and with men. For him the nine muses sing for all life.

First hymn they the Father
Of all things; and then,
The rest of immortals,
The action of men.

The day in his hotness,
The strife with the palm;
The night in her silence,
The stars in their calm.

The three attitudes toward nature dramatized in the poem take, at last, their extreme forms. The least interesting and perhaps the most sensible is that of Pausanias, the attitude of the practical scientist who would learn the secrets of nature in order to use them for immediate human ends. Empedocles, the philosopher, has the most to say about his, a noble view, perhaps, if one that allows for suicide.[13] Callicles takes the attitude of the poet who finds beauty and even solace in nature, who believes in gods at least while he is singing, and who unites man with the environment as the foreground and the background of a picture. For all its length, and the dull stretch in the first act is very long, the poem adds up to an impressive pres-

13. Arnold later pointed to Empedocles' suicide as evidence that the character is not simply speaking his creator's thoughts (see Tinker and Lowry, p. 287), but the philosophical passages of the poem are too familiar in substance not to sound like echoes and partial voices of the poet's own more Stoic or Senecan mind.

Tinker and Lowry remark the influence of Carlyle on Arnold in this poem (p. 300), an influence that is probably greater here and elsewhere than either the poet or some of his critics have supposed. It is, however, amusing to observe the poet calling the old prophet a moral desperado and Carlyle complaining that Arnold is "taking no part in God's work" but fiddling while Rome burns. See *Letters . . . to Clough*, p. 111; Houghton, *The Victorian Frame of Mind*, p. 247n; and Kathleen Tillotson, "Matthew Arnold and Carlyle," *Proceedings of the British Academy, 43* (1956), 133–53.

entation of these attitudes: impressive partly because it allows for dialogue, for a single grand action, and for a striking contrast between philosopher and poet. It is not consistently in Arnold's best vein, and it is not a dramatic whole with an explicit resolution, but "Empedocles" is, among the poet's verse criticisms of ideas, the most brilliantly sustained. How telling the criticism was and how discordant with his later views the poet indicated by withdrawing it in 1853 as too painful.

Again, as in "The Forsaken Merman," Arnold has created polar figures that define his own extremes. If Empedocles' speech is a "dialogue of the mind with itself," there is a dialogue, too, between Empedocles and Callicles, between Arnold as a critical thinker and Arnold as a strayed reveller, a seer and singer of the things purer imagination sees. Unable to sustain the voice and view of Empedocles, and unable fully to resolve the tension between criticism and mythic imagination in a series of dramatic actions, to create characters capable of acting positively in the world of men as well as suffering deeply, Arnold can at least—or at best—visualize and give a limited dramatic form to these disparities.

Some of his most valuable poems, including "The Forsaken Merman," "Dover Beach" and "Tristram and Iseult," do only that. They are not poetic drama, but they are dramatic poems in which monologue and dialogue are used to embody tensions within the mind or between minds and ways of viewing life, tensions that prophets or playwrights might have to resolve. The tableau, the moment of insight, the all but tragic acceptance, the elegiac mood, are what Arnold's most steady vision concentrates upon and what his surest voice speaks.

# 5. The Voice of the Narrator

WHETHER IT TAKES the form of soliloquy, of monologue, or of dialogue, virtually all of Arnold's best poetry involves, then, what he calls in his Preface of 1853 the "dialogue of the mind with itself." This process, Arnold asserts, had commenced by the time of the historical Empedocles, and apparently it continues in the minds of modern men; for, unlike a Platonic dialogue, the conversation of inner voices does not often conclude with the wisdom of one master voice. Arnold's dialogue between disillusioned Tristram and faithful Iseult and his contrast between the songs of Empedocles and those of Callicles make these several voices seem to represent the several sides of a dialogue, as it were, within the poet's own mind, just as the opposites of land and sea do in "The Forsaken Merman" and "Dover Beach." But, perhaps because literal dialogue can so easily be reduced to unsettled debate on points of philosophy and religion, as it is in Clough's "Dipsychus," or to simple preaching, as it begins to be in the first act of "Empedocles," the dialogue of the poet's mind with itself is often represented less strikingly in the speeches of his characters than in contrasts implied by the more indirect and symbolic means.

In Arnold's narrative poetry, too, the inner tensions are realized by contrasts in imagery and setting, along with the speeches that reveal the differences between Sohrab and Rustum or between Balder and his fellows. Although the weaker narratives, like "Saint Brandan," amount at last to fairly single-minded moralities, the most successful of Arnold's poetic tales involve these contrasts and are essentially double visions. The voice of the narrator does not intrude upon the stories as it does sometimes in "Tristram"—where the pronouns *I, we,* and *you* introduce the author's and the reader's points of view and where, in the third part, a moralizing *I* comments directly on the poem—but it describes actions and settings so as to reveal differences not only between several people's lives but also between several ways of viewing their lives.

The views implied, the messages carried, in "The Neckan" and "Saint Brandan" are comparatively simple: each of these short narratives versifies a folk tale which shows that there may be divine grace given to one who is apparently lost. The first piece is another version of the tale that Arnold tells in "The Forsaken Merman," but now the story is rendered almost as a ballad, and in the third person; and, although the words of the sea-creature are again plaintive, his attitude, that of his wife, and the implicit attitude of the narrator are much less painfully ambivalent than those in the better poem. The neckan accepts the values of the land, if only for the woman's sake, for he asks to be signed by the cross. The wife, again unseen, but hardly so sympathetic a person as Margaret, can only weep because her mate is no Christian but a creature of the sea; and it seems that even the miracle which makes a priest's staff bud and branch, as a sign that the neckan can be saved, does not change her reticence and her husband's sadness. A quatrain added to the poem in 1869 (the original was published in 1853) takes emphasis away from the miracle to make this point explicit:

> He said: 'The earth hath kindness,
>     The sea, the starry poles;
> Earth, sea, and sky, and God above—
>     But, ah, not human souls!'

The mood of these lines is almost directly opposed to that of "Dover Beach," where the earth is seen to lack the sympathy that human love may provide. But this poem is not, like "Dover Beach," qualified by any imagery in contrast to its message: it never makes us feel strongly why the earth and his mate are so attractive to the neckan, and so it realizes only one side of the contrast between the natural and the human orders. The difference, however, between "The Neckan" and some other less impressive poems is that the Christian God now seems to be on the side of this lonely creature who is more human than the human beings in his sadness, not that of the smug priest, the horrified knights and ladies and the weeping wife. And that difference, after all, helps to give interest to this rather tight and limited version of the pathetic story.

"Saint Brandan," too, Arnold's verse rendering of the Celtic legend about Judas on the iceberg, carries some interest as evidence of the poet's desire to make the most of the most humane elements in religion. It is a crisply told tale of the Saint's vision on the "sea without a human shore," a vision of the archtraitor momentarily relieved from his torment each Christmas eve because of one good deed done in his lifetime. But these stanzas, which include dialogue within the narrative (and Judas' narrative within his speech), are less dramatic than parabolic, are simple and fanciful rather than complex and serious. Arnold does not allow his own mixed feelings to enter into the telling of this folk tale as, for instance, Thomas Hardy does in his sadly skeptical lines about another popular tale of wonderful occurrences each Christmas eve, "The Oxen." Arnold's poem can too easily be summed up: "That germ of kindness, in the womb/ Of mercy caught, [does] not expire."

It is not so easy to sum up the sense of his longer narrative "The Church of Brou," a poem that lacks the richness of Arnold's greatest verse tales but one that has, nevertheless, some fine passages, especially in the last part. Although this work is not included by the poet among his "Narrative Poems"—the category into which, strange to say, Arnold puts "The Forsaken Merman," along with "The Sick King in Bokhara" and "Tristram and Iseult"—it is a clearer narrative (if a poorer poem) than "Tristram," to which, as Tinker and Lowry observe, it bears some resemblance.[1] Like "The Neckan," "The Church of Brou" must suffer by comparison with the larger work it resembles; but the contrast is not now so distinct or even so extreme. In this poem, as in "Tristram and Iseult," there are three parts, the last consisting of a static scene. The strictly narrative section, the first, is easily the weakest, a rapid account of the young Duke's death which tosses off, in its gallop from stanza to stanza, such hurried lines as "Hark! a shout—a crash—a groan!" and "Senseless, weltering in his gore." The second part, describing the church built by Duchess Marguerite, is very much subtler in rhythm and diction. And the final section (printed separately in 1877), imagining the princely pair as they might awake in their marble tombs, is by far the finest passage in the poem.

> Then, gazing up 'mid the dim pillars high,
> The foliaged marble forest where ye lie,
> *Hush*, ye will say, *it is eternity!*
> *This is the glimmering verge of Heaven, and these*
> *The columns of the heavenly palaces!*

1. In their commentary, p. 37 and pp. 115–16.

Here is another transformation by the poet of the grave into a greenwood, of death into peace, of cold marble and darkness into a sense of enchantment in the kindly light of fantasy, some such transformation as is achieved, in other ways, by "Balder Dead" and "Sohrab and Rustum."

"Balder Dead," a poem obviously comparable with "Sohrab and Rustum"—Arnold compared the two and preferred "Balder," although his readers have rarely done so—brings more complication into its storytelling than "Sohrab" and departs somewhat more from its source in its ordering of events and use of narrative detail. If it is not quite so fine a poem as the more celebrated work, "Balder" nevertheless makes a better narrative, with its beginning *in medias res,* its omens and foreshadowings, journeys and quests. It adapts a Homeric manner and an ultimately Virgilian tone to another kind of classical material, the Norse, dealing with an heroic society and with the death of a hero: "Balder" begins as "Sohrab and Rustum" ends, with the death of and the mourning for a mighty father's mighty son. But "Balder" makes more use of dialogue between characters, so that it is rather more vigorous and less stately in its diction and movement. And this extended journey into the underworld provides a more nearly direct comment upon its own world —a more nearly direct rejection of strife in favor of peace, in favor perhaps of death. Even so, the Eddic poem is ultimately like "Sohrab," again, in that it displays and does not easily dismiss two views of what the best of worlds, the best of lives, would be.

In fact, "Balder" is a poem of polarities, of ironies and even of paradoxes. It is filled with a visionary knowledge of the future— the knowledge that Frea possesses and Odin, and finally Balder too —which makes its action seem inevitably futile, and yet the gods are apparently fated to will and act against the decrees of fatality. Its central figure is the ideal hero of a Valhalla to whose heroic code he is opposed. And its imagery again and again contrasts the value of heavenly warfare with the value of heavenly rest.

To the tensions implicit within this dark story the narration gives emphasis, especially in its use of imagery. First, there is a contrast between epic characters, setting, and movement, all of which are magnified and formal, and the details that give a specific, even personal, quality to the poem. This contrast is enforced almost always by the Homeric similes, which Arnold introduces with reference neither to Homer nor to the Edda. Hoder's touch on Hermod's arm is like the touch of honeysuckle brushing across a tired traveler's face (surely English honeysuckle and an English traveler), and the road to Hell is blocked by a maiden just as a mountain pass is blocked by cattle. The familiar epic device is used in this way frequently enough to make the gods of the story seem earthly in their experience as well as their tempers. Lok, in the guise of the hag Thok, jeers at his fellow gods and compares them to cows leaving their hay as they roam the world, asking all things to weep for Balder. Here, by the way, the extended simile is spoken by a character; and in a comparable passage, Lok belittles both Hermod and Balder by comparing one with a farmer and the other with the farmer's lost and pitiful dog. In each of these passages, a human feeling of weakness and pathos is given to the situation of the warlike gods.

But it is not only through the epic similes, with their yoking of heroic events and pastoral or domestic terms, that the Eddic story takes on its new dimensions. Images and themes that are symbolic and recurrent in Arnold's poetry, those of light and shadow, of battle in life and repose in death, are embodied in the settings and metaphors of this poem, and they again express duality, tension, or dialogue between contrasting attitudes. The most striking contrast, perhaps, is that between the dark and the sunlit places. There is daylight in Heaven, and none in the place of obscure spirits; Odin would, on entering Hell, "set the fields of gloom ablaze with light," did not Frea insist that he could not rightly violate Hela's darkness. Both Thok's iron wood and Hela's world are dark, cold regions, and their shadows are associated with the dreary and morbid. And yet the brilliance of Odin's Asgard is a harsh brilliance, one that is not at last so clearly preferable to the peaceful gloom of Hela. For, in his last speech, Arnold's Balder, no longer simply a Norse god, is minded to accept the surcease from strife that is death, and he declares to his fellow god,

> I am long since weary of your storm
> Of carnage, and find, Hermod, in your life
> Something too much of war and broils, which make
> Life one perpetual fight, a bath of blood.
> Mine eyes are dizzy with the arrowy hail;
> Mine ears are stunn'd with blows, and sick for calm.
> Inactive therefore let me lie, in gloom,
> Unarm'd, inglorious.

Not that the gloom is final, for he continues,

>                           I attend the course
> Of ages, and my late return to light,
> In times less alien to a spirit mild,
> In new-recover'd seats, the happier day.'

>          .      .      .

> 'Far to the south, beyond the blue, there spreads
> Another Heaven, the boundless—no one yet
> Hath reach'd it; there hereafter shall arise
> The second Asgard, with another name.

> Thither, when o'er this present earth and Heavens
> The tempest of the latter days hath swept,
> And they from sight have disappear'd, and sunk,
> Shall a small remnant of the Gods repair;
> Hoder and I shall join them from the grave.
> There re-assembling we shall see emerge
> From the bright Ocean at our feet an earth
> More fresh, more verdant than the last, with fruits
> Self-springing, and a seed of man preserved,
> Who then shall live in peace, as now in war.[2]

This promise of a paradise divine and human is a glowing one, one that combines light with peace. But for now Balder is willing to accept the peace of darkness.

The final paradox of the poem has to do with the nature of death. Within the hall where heroes live after their valiant deaths, a god has died, only to find rest in his underworld and to anticipate a new life. The name of the poem and its first lines introduce us to the subject of life in death—we never see Balder *alive,* literally, but he is quite as alive in another sense as any of the gods—and the titles of its parts remind us of it. Like "Tristram" and "The Church of Brou," the narrative has a threefold division, with sections called "Sending," "Journey to the Dead," and "Funeral." The task that Hermod is sent upon is the recovery of Balder from the realm of ghosts, the mythical quest of Orpheus, but his journey is to be vain, for the guile of Lok the enemy, who caused Balder's downfall

---

2. The Eddic *Völuspá* includes such a prediction of the new world to rise after Asgard is destroyed, and the prediction has led some scholars to postulate a Christian influence upon the poem (and a date of composition not much before the year 1000); but there is nothing in the Poetic Edda to suggest that the vision is Balder's or that he is such a seer and gentle spirit as he becomes in Arnold's version.

by giving blind Hoder the mistletoe to throw at him, prevents the gods from meeting Hela's demand that all things grieve for Balder before he be returned to life. And so the god's funeral, with his ship a pyre sent blazing out to sea, is for Asgard final, if not for Balder. The most nearly invincible of the gods, after Odin himself, seems at last to be subject to death's power, and not only in the body but in his mind and will. Arnold's version of the story, filled with forebodings and ominous signs of a Götterdämmerung, suggests some promise too, through Balder's vision of a new Heaven and a new earth, but it concludes literally in darkness and withdrawal, not only with life in death but with a sense of death in life—or, rather, with a melancholy sense of how imperfect, in the world as it is, both energy without peace and peace without energy must be.

Balder's vision of peace and wholeness, then, the Arnoldian vision, is only that, a vision of the longed-for future. Even the god's acceptance of his death cannot make us forget the contrast, the opposition, at the heart of the poem between darkness and light, between the pathetic picture of life as essentially passive, resigned at best to the inevitable, and the picture of an heroic existence as a series of quests or battles which the gods delight to watch if not to enter. The underworld is a place of shadows, but Asgard is filled with endless warfare. The vision of a new Heaven may enchant us, and Hermod too, but for the time being, as he leaves the ghostly Balder in his dreary home by the northern sea, the fleet god must return to a city of futile battles. Neither Hell nor Heaven seems at last to be quite satisfactory, as neither sea nor land is in "The Forsaken Merman." For if death is not final, then life itself is not final or full, and even a Heavenly version of this life is imperfect; the last lines of the poem suggest Hermod's realization of that truth, when, so humanly weak as to seem like a poor trapped bird, he longs for a moment to stay in the gloom with his fellow gods but must return instead to the wearisome fields of light. His longing to remain with Balder in darkness is expressed by the fancied bird's longing to fly toward the sunlit south, the south where, we recall, Balder's new Asgard will be.

> And as a stork which idle boys have trapp'd,
> And tied him in a yard, at autumn sees
> Flocks of his kind pass flying o'er his head
> To warmer lands, and coasts that keep the sun;—
> He strains to join their flight, and from his shed
> Follows them with a long complaining cry—
> So Hermod gazed, and yearn'd to join his kin.

> At last he sigh'd, and set forth back to Heaven.

The paradox of "Balder Dead," that the pagan Hell offers peace with gloom and the heroic Heaven weariness with glory, is very closely related to an ironic quality of "Sohrab and Rustum," in which two images of human existence are even more clearly opposed one to the other. Partly because "Sohrab and Rustum" has a somewhat less complex plot and partly, perhaps, because it ends with the narrator's description of a scene rather than a character's speech, the effect of the work is more formal and "poetic"; but in its exploiting of the subject, involving a conflict of father and son, and in its extensive use of imagery both Homeric and symbolic, "Sohrab" finally achieves, if less rapidity, then an even more moving effect of pathos than "Balder Dead."

Implicit in Arnold's Persian material is the psychological significance of a son's search for his father and the battle between the two, followed by reconciliation. No doubt the poet's own feelings as the son of a famous father are reflected in his choice of this story about Sohrab's defeat by Rustum (Sohrab is in effect defeated by his filial piety, for it is his father's name that vanquishes him): at least that assumption is consistent with the notation by Wyndham Slade to the effect that "The Voice" in Arnold's poem of that title, the voice that the speaker resists although it moves him, is his father's—and with Auden's assertion that Thomas Arnold's earnest voice finally destroyed the poet in his son.[3] But presumably the son and poet was not fully aware of his motive in choosing this material. Just as it is possible for the action in the poem to occur because father and son do not recognize each other, so it is possible for Arnold to narrate the action, and the death of the young warrior, because he has not fully recognized Sohrab and Rustum, because the conflict does not have to be presented as a distinct and personal irreconciliation of old earnestness and young enthusiasm.

Even so, the death of Sohrab is painful, and the fair amount of skill Arnold displays in using narrative devices of irony (Rustum's "Be as a son to me," for instance) and fore-shadowing (as in the initial scene between Sohrab and the paternal Peran-Wisa, who predicts "danger or death") might not be enough to make the finest poetry of this pattern that is so painfully resolved—at least, not according to the critical doctrine that led Arnold to withdraw his "Empedocles." The most striking parts of the poem, striking because of their conjunction with the narrative, are those metaphorical and symbolic passages that once more transform violence into beauty and death into peace; one is likely to remember these pictures rather than the intermittent dialogue or the details of the main action. And these pictures of suffering and death, of living in strife and dying in peace, suggest again the tension between two ways of seeing man's situation, between the epic temper that glorifies heroic strife, and the philosophical or even religious attitude that would subdue the individual to Fate and Nature.

"Sohrab and Rustum" makes somewhat more extensive use of

3. See Tinker and Lowry, p. 49, for the notation on "The Voice."

the Homeric simile than "Balder," again with the effect of adding immediacy and pathos to the military events of the poem; at the same time, the similes provide relief from and dramatic contrast to the tension which gradually builds up all the way through the first half of the poem. And so the imagery, rather like that of the *Iliad,* often evokes scenes basically unlike those of camp and battle, recalling either peaceful settings from nature or domestic life. In presenting a dramatic moment, Arnold turns to the cornfield and the mountain:

> As, in the country, on a morn in June,
> When the dew glistens on the pearled ears,
> A shiver runs through the deep corn for joy—
> So, when they heard what Peran-Wisa said,
> A thrill through all the Tartar squadrons ran
> Of pride and hope for Sohrab, whom they loved.

> But as a troop of pedlars, from Cabool,
> Cross underneath the Indian Caucasus,
> That vast sky-neighbouring mountain of milk snow;
> Crossing so high, that, as they mount, they pass
> Long flocks of travelling birds dead on the snow,
> Choked by the air, and scarce can they themselves
> Slake their parch'd throats with sugar'd mulberries—
> In single file they move, and stop their breath,
> For fear they should dislodge the o'erhanging snows—
> So the pale Persians held their breath with fear.

Of course these similes may also reflect the feelings of participants in the action, especially when their substance is oriental. Other such extended or Homeric similes compare files of soldiers with cranes; Rustum surveying Sohrab with a rich woman curiously eying a poor drudge; Rustum's figure with a lonely tower in the waste; Rustum's club with a tree trunk fished from a flooded river; Rustum's uneasy incredulity when Sohrab claims to be his son with the uneasy feeling of the eagle whose mate lies slain far away. The space given to the literal description of the second term in each simile, of the cranes, the woman peering through a curtain, the tree trunk in the river, the eagle circling his nest, makes each one an excursion from the narrative into another, a small but vivid, poetic world. Only the image of the woman is distinctly unrelated to the area of experience and the physical area in which the battle takes place, and like the others it characterizes by indirection. Just as Rustum is compared with the tower in a waste and the noble but baffled eagle, there is something in him also of the proud and curious figure—feminine in both vain pride and curiosity—who lives in another world from the one inhabited by those around him.

Perhaps the two most striking epic similes are those which compare the dying Sohrab with a flower, first with a hyacinth and then with a violet—similes that may remind us of the deaths both of Gorgythion in the *Iliad,* whose head droops in death like a poppy, and of Euryalus in the *Aeneid.* The device works well for Arnold as it has for Homer and Virgil, and the images are strangely beautiful. They are, of course, in extreme contrast with the literal scene, for they draw our attention from the plain which has become a scene of death to the cultivated garden, where flowers are destroyed merely by carelessness. Both similes occur after the tension of the conflict has been suddenly relaxed, while Sohrab is slowly dying, and they do not follow the tendency that has made the earlier images reflect the minds of actors within the poem, leaping to pictures of cranes and eagles, Caucasus mountains and Persian deserts; the feeling of the similes becomes less subjective now as it becomes less violent. Finally, the contrast between images of flowers and the idea of battle and bloody death is a way of turning death into a beautiful event: the image transforms a human agony into what is objectively seen as a graceful if not even a glorious consummation.[4]

The sense of death as consummation is yet more beautifully embodied in the water imagery of the poem. The whole scene, the challenge, the fierce battle, and the death of Sohrab, has taken place by the river Oxus, which is alluded to again and again, even in the midst of the fighting. Near the end Sohrab speaks of "the yellow Oxus, by whose brink I die," and Rustum replies,

> 'Oh that its waves were flowing over me!
> Oh, that I saw its grains of yellow silt
> Roll tumbling in the current o'er my head!'

But he must live; as Sohrab predicts, with the vision of the dying, Rustum may not find the peace of death until he returns "home over the salt blue sea, / From laying thy dear master in his grave." "Soon be that day," the father says, "and deep that sea!" Again, the sea suggests death and peace, and the inevitable. In an earlier passage Sohrab has said,

> We are all, like swimmers in the sea,
> Poised on the top of a huge wave of fate,
> Which hangs uncertain to which side to fall.
> And whether it will heave us up to land,
> Or whether it will roll us out to sea,
> Back out to sea, to the deep waves of death,
> We know not.

Even in the detail of Sohrab's drawing forth the spear there is a sug-

4. For a comment on this effect, see Kenneth Burke, *A Rhetoric of Motives* (New York, 1950), pp. 7–10.

gestion of Arnold's favorite images, the stream of life and the sea of death:

> the blood
> Came welling from the open gash, and life
> Flow'd with the stream.

Finally, the sense of moving through life toward death, toward fulfillment, is embodied in the picture of the Oxus and the ocean: in the night, as Sohrab lies dead, the river flows on, away from this plain where the battles of human life are fought, where heat and strife and pain disturb its course, through sands and rushes, slowly but steadily, until

> at last
> The long'd for dash of waves is heard, and wide
> His luminous home of waters opens, bright
> And tranquil, from whose floor the new-bathed stars
> Emerge, and shine upon the Aral Sea.

This ending, in exalted calm after struggle, is the finest thing in the poem.

Just as the metaphors are fine only in the context of the narrative, however, this last passage of description gains its power from the terrible and finally pathetic events that precede it. We know that the old warrior has defeated himself in defeating his enemy, and we have seen a poignant outcome of the conflict between generations. With the change of mood from urgent vigor to quiet grief, from heroic to elegiac, the poem concludes in what might be called a brief comment of the narrator's—but a comment made by indirection—which reveals another way of viewing this action. Now a new contrast is implied, between the story of two human lives reaching their climax in the battle of ignorant forces on a darkling plain and the imaging forth of human life as essentially a natural flowing of waters toward their consummation in the ultimate and inevitable sea. Two opposed views of what man's world is like are suggested, but only suggested, here. The last lines of "Dover Beach," setting these same two views one against the other, escape from seeming too flatly oracular because they remain dramatic, and because in them the powerful rhythm of the ocean that is denied as a relevant symbol can still be heard, insistent. Now, the symbolic conclusion to the narrative is equally effective because it acts by indirection. It need not state that the natural world is an alien battlefield where fierce men struggle their meaningless lives away, nor that the reality of nature is an ocean in which every man is a current controlled by a greater power. With a strangely fine effect, Arnold superimposes his transcendental imagery of the waters, an imagery that in itself may seem too transcendental to be striking, and too familiar as well, upon his starkly simple Persian tale; and so we feel at once the terror and the peace, the ironic bitterness and the strange beauty, of Sohrab's death.

In "Sohrab and Rustum," as in "Balder Dead," the contrasts are implicit in action, speech, and setting: the dialogue of the mind with itself is represented but does not become a debate. The narrator of "Balder" makes no specific comment on the Eddic values that his transcription of the story must reveal when the inhabitants of Hell are described as women, cowards, and old men who had the misfortune to die in bed rather than in battle; but the final mood of Balder is comment enough. Again, the boasting of Rustum and Sohrab's love of strife are reflected upon not by the voice of the poet but by the irony of events and by the last image in the poem. These narratives retain their interest and power partly because Arnold has been able in adapting the classical material to represent some such inner tensions as have presumably characterized the western mind at least from the time of Greeks like Empedocles, and to do so without simply moralizing on his tales or modernizing them and limiting their significance to specifically Victorian problems. Arnold is like some other Victorian poets in drawing largely from mythical and legendary materials for his narrative poems, and his plotting of these materials is less masterly than Tennyson's or even Morris's; in his ability to translate legendary scenes into not only contemporary terms but timeless human situations, however, he far surpasses Morris and easily rivals Tennyson. "Balder Dead" is infused with a moving quality that the more truly Eddic "Sigurd the Volsung" rarely achieves, and "Tristram and Iseult" is a more beautiful poem than any of the *Idylls*. One might go so far, indeed, as to compare the death of Balder favorably with the more thrilling but very slightly stagy death of Arthur.

Although narrative invention is not his *forte* and his production of strictly narrative verse is slight, Arnold can, in the last of "Tristram" and especially in "Balder Dead" and "Sohrab and Rustum," add even to good stories a heightening and enriching quality that is peculiarly his own: a quality of pathos deep and genuine and touched at best with a sense of the dignity of human suffering. His double vision, of men and gods as heroic forces, and of Nature or Fate as the single dominant principle in the life of the world, reflects two sides, two voices, of his imagination: voices that can fairly be represented if not perfectly reconciled in the action and imagery of these poems, in the one voice of the narrator.

# 6. Arnold as a Living Poet

ARNOLD'S GROUNDS for passing literary judgment are so various that we can hardly speak in a general way of applying his own critical principles to his poetry. In his comment on "Empedocles" and now and then in his letters he suggests the purely pragmatic view that justifies a poem according to its effect on the mind and spirits of the reader; he is concerned, so to speak, with the function of poetry at the present time. This concern seems to motivate his famous prediction that poetry will come more and more to replace dogmatic religion. It does not, perhaps, allow for a very favorable judgment of "Dover Beach" and several other melancholy works.

But his most famous prescriptive definition of poetry would make it a "criticism of life," in a phrase that is ambiguous enough to have been given several interpretations.[1] Apparently Arnold himself interprets the idea at different times in different ways: for instance, in "The World and the Quietist," where the poet is represented as debating and blaming, as explicitly commenting upon the world's activity, and in the "Epilogue" to Lessing, where the bard's first

---

1. Lionel Trilling takes the phrase in a very broad and sophisticated sense, as Arnold does sometimes, no doubt; but the essay on "The Study of Poetry" leaves it fairly vague. See Trilling's *Matthew Arnold*, pp. 194–6.

loyalty is to his vision of the whole tendency of Life, a vision that only implies critical judgment on petty, partial, and eccentric lives. In either sense, it is difficult to say how some of Arnold's best poetry is a criticism of life, as distinct from implicit criticism of ideas about life.

Occasionally, however, as in his "Caution to Poets," Arnold suggests the Romantic idea that poetry is valuable only when it expresses the most genuine feelings of its creator. Perhaps he tries to follow his own advice, too, but we can hardly know, and parts of "Rugby Chapel" may make us wonder. On the other hand, his insistence upon the classical objectivity of the poetic work is quite another criterion, one which our critics are likely to find more sympathetic than his pragmatic, visionary, and Romantic ways of judging. It is, nevertheless, a criterion of which "The Grande Chartreuse" and even "Tristram and Iseult" might be said to fall short.

Finally, there is Arnold's "touchstone" method of criticism, a device rather than a standard. If we were to apply that method to his work, we could cite the last few lines of such poems as "Shakespeare," the "Gipsy Child," "The Forsaken Merman," "Sohrab and Rustum," "Tristram and Iseult," and "Dover Beach," lines which evoke man's grief and majesty, his weakness and courage, the forces of conquering death and urgent love; or we might serve Arnold as he serves the Augustans, and quote the opening of "To A Friend," or "The Austerity of Poetry."

This cavalier summing-up, from a jumble of sources, of Arnold's various critical approaches, is of course unfair to him as a critic, for it distorts his opinion by giving equal weight to hints and disquisitions, and it ignores all subtleties. Of course, too, there are senses in which almost all of these criteria can be adduced for praising many passages in his poetry—passages that may well move, even exalt us, that may certainly enlarge our conceptions and have the effect of criticizing our partial easy notions about life, passages apparently filled with the intense emotion of the poet even as they embody the formal control of emotion we sometimes think of as classical. And yet, if we apply Arnold's critical ideas strictly, any one of these approaches to the judgment of poems could be taken to show that the poet's best work is badly flawed, is dubious in large part. In fact, Arnold's criticism, fine as it can be, is almost never directed toward the kind of poetry of which he is master, a poetry not of positive philosophy or of positive actions, but one of mixed feeling given objective form.

A strictly historical estimate, the kind against which Arnold warns in his essay on the study of poetry, might seem to do him more honor than any based upon his own explicit views. The comment on his writing that he made to his mother has, we now understand, a prophetic ring: "My poems represent, on the whole, the main movement of mind of the last quarter of a century, and thus they will probably have their day as people become conscious to themselves of what that movement of mind is, and interested in the literary productions which reflect it."[2] Still, interest in literary productions only as reflections of the times is not a strictly literary interest, as the critical Arnold rightly insists—although this is an important fact about a writer, that he realizes the intellectual currents of his day, and a fact with which some of Arnold's most intelligent commentators have been concerned.

The best case for Matthew Arnold's relevance to the present day has been made by Lionel Trilling, who describes and demonstrates Arnold's critical temper of mind. Professor Trilling deals with the man's ideas and ideals—ideals of order, of balance, of lucid and reasonable judgment, of, in a word, wholeness; and because both

2. *Letters of Matthew Arnold 1848–1888,* ed. George W. E. Russell, *2* (New York, 1896), 10.

Arnold's ideas and his ideals, held up for men and for classes of men, find expression in his poetry, Trilling's case is in part a case for the poetry. But it is not a case for the poetry as poetry. Importantly as ideas are involved in the structure of any poem, and especially of a poem written by the most intellectual poet of his time, they are involved in various ways; they do not define the poem so much as they are qualified and defined by it. The case for Arnold as a living force in the world of ideas is not the whole case for Arnold as an artist.

Arnold's poetry has sometimes been judged as poetry, of course, most recently by Kenneth Allott in a sensitive and frankly personal defense of the poet as "the most congenial" of the Victorians.[3] But if we are to be more precise than that, and if we cannot accept any one of Arnold's own criteria as quite adequate, we must finally arrive at a formulation of the grounds for judgments already made or implied. The value of Arnold's poetry, we might say, consists in the degree of steadiness and wholeness, to use his language, and of adequacy to serious human experience which is achieved in a number of poems, including "Dover Beach," "The Forsaken Merman," "Tristram and Iseult," and, perhaps slightly less close to perfect integrity, "To a Gipsy Child," and "Sohrab and Rustum." Assuming that no very serious human experiences involve the simplest reactions to simple facts, each of these poems must be taken to include some complexity, some divers strains and straining within its unity if it is said to be adequate; as for "serious" experience, the term is not meant to exclude the comic or comic admixtures, which are in fact missing in Arnold (possibly he is a narrower and lesser poet for the lack), or to suggest "high seriousness" in his sense of the phrase, but only to rule out what is simply topical and trivial. "Geist's

---

3. In his introduction to the "Penguin Poets" selection of Arnold (Baltimore, 1954), p. 10.

Grave," "Poor Matthias," and "Kaiser Dead" represent some pleasant enough versifying; the "Sonnet to the Hungarian Nation" is not even that. Wholeness of treatment and seriousness of subject probably amount to the same thing at last (in Pope, trivia are transformed in that the steady and whole view of trivia is by no means trivial) because, wholly understood, all human experience is probably complex and serious; but it is useful to keep both terms, both wholeness and seriousness, as Arnold himself might prefer to do. When he warns Clough against trying to solve the universe, Arnold is aware of the thinness and partiality which are likely to mark universal "solutions," so inadequate to their absolutely serious object. When he complains of Tennyson's dawdling with the painted shell of the universe, he knows that formal completeness is illusory without a serious matter.

From the days of his dandyish youth to his eminent middle age, Arnold is inclined to take serious problems for his subjects, and our complaint about his dealing with these problems does not concern the solemnity of the subjects but rather his hesitation or simple pomposity of tone and the incompleteness of his treatment. Time and again his work seems thin and partial, not whole and decided. When he preaches dogma Arnold loses his poet's voice, for he has neither the fixed Weltanschauung to give it conviction nor the ability to suspend the doubts he feels. Happily, at least, he is not long willing, like a versifying Carlyle, to shout down his own misgivings.

But when Arnold speaks in soliloquy that sufficiently clarifies his vacillating mind, in the poetic *I* that implies no demanding *you,* no audience to edify, he can achieve at least a personal integrity. And when he speaks in monologue he can, at best, give objective form to his sense of man's alienation from and conflict with his environment. By using dramatic and fictional means, too, he can reveal a double vision in the contrasts between the voices of men, or between the voice of the actor and that of the narrator. If there is a danger of his oracles' being unconvincing and his soliloquies too indecisive, the poet who lives between two worlds, the poet of two minds, is true by indirect means to his imagination: when Arnold's poetry embodies the inner dialogue of his mind it recognizes the tyranny of time and yet asserts an order that transcends all temporal change; it celebrates both the society of human beings, with its bond of love, and the longing for a buried life, for isolation from the noisy crowd of others; it praises natural force and the idea of Nature, and it sees steadily the danger to humanity of natural coldness, natural strength.

A double mind is one mark of the age; it is often expressed in self-consciousness and the self-critical uncertainty that leads to hero-worship and the straining for oracular voices, so that Victorian poetry is liable to be either prophetic and obscure or, as Mill would have it, "overheard." But Arnold is a somewhat special instance in being aware of these matters, in refusing, at least, to be overheard playing parts for the sake of talking in some remarkable way, and in insisting upon the ideal of integrity, of a whole view, which he can achieve only by the yoking of opposites. In spite of his misgivings about the intellect's overlaying and crushing "poetical expression," his best work is more nearly perfected because a half-enchanted intelligence forms it from below, stirring in and under its poetic form: because of his critical intelligence, seeing life whole means for him grasping that *porro unum est necessarium*—it means seeing paradoxes, complications, irreducible antinomies he can express in vision, in metaphor and dialogue.

Tennyson has visions, too, but they seem to be impressive only when they are freed from the control of strong ideas, when they are divorced from and even opposed to the poet's thinking. With

Arnold there is always much more interplay of mind and fancy. Whereas his prose criticism uses rhetorical and "poetic" devices to persuade, his poetry is in some ways less inspirational and more truly critical than the prose—more stringently critical of ideas and their implications. But this criticism is indirect, and it involves the feelings along with the intelligence. In fact, for all his abstract language, Arnold's is an imaginative, a "feeling" intelligence: he is not often either witty or incisive, even in his prose. And he is always at least half aware, as we must be, that his most literal-sounding lines about greenwoods and battleplains, sunlight and shadow, dry land and sea, have to do with the persistent question of man's relation to the mysterious world of nature which he fears and worships, controls and serves; with the questions of man's relation to other men, his isolation from or identity with his fellows, and of man's relation to himself, of the alienation of his consciousness from his innermost being.

His dialogue between poet and critic results in momentary steadiness as well as wholeness, in the control of tone without which poems are not consistent and whole, when Arnold retains but submerges his conflicting (or at least contrasting) ideas and impulses about such matters in the forms of fiction, drama, and imagery: when his voice is that not of the poetic critic but of the profoundly and subtly critical poet. It is then that he reconciles the several voices, the several minds, with which most intelligent Victorians, and fragmented modern men as well, must speak.

# Index

*This book was designed by Crimilda Pontes,*
*set in Aldine Bembo type, with hand-lettered titles,*
*and printed by the Carl Purington Rollins Printing-Office*
*of the Yale University Press, New Haven, Connecticut*